ADVENTUR

Duran

PETE

ADVENTURES WITH

Durango
PETE

Life and
Poetry with
a Cow Dog
Philsofur

STEPHEN HINMAN

Adventures with Durango Pete:
Life and Poetry with a Cow Dog Philosfur
Published by Barking Crow Publishing
Littleton, CO 80125

Library of Congress Control Number: 2017946109

ISBN: 978-0-9985639-0-9

PETS / Essays & Narratives

Cover Design by Victoria Wolf

QUANTITY PURCHASES: Schools, companies, professional
groups, clubs, and other organizations may qualify for special
terms when ordering quantities of this title. For information, email
info@BarkingCrowPublishing.com.

BARKING CROW
PUBLISHING

This book is dedicated to my mother.
Her abiding love and kindness inform all
my earthly undertakings. She is the angel
on my shoulder and I miss her every day.

Introduction

EVERYBODY WHO HAS A DOG thinks his or her canine pal is the greatest. That is the way it should be. I get it. No arguments. So, I ask you to humor me and afford me the same luxury—or delusion. I want to tell you about a dog who is my sidekick and share a few stories and observations about life that I discovered—or recovered—thanks to Durango Pete, a crazy cattle dog who was born in New Mexico, relinquished for adoption at the tender age of six weeks, saved by a great lady, and a short-time later, came to live with me and my wife in Colorado.

But this story is not simply the tale of a man gushing about what a great dog he has as a companion. It is really the story about two souls, both on their own journeys, and the gifts they gave each other along the way. All of us have dreams, fears, needs, anxieties, and curiosity. Durango Pete, I discovered, is no different. We all have unique perspectives and gifts to share. We all want to be appreciated, needed, loved. Often, the darkness that is part of us stands in the way of our light manifesting. Our fears—expressed as insecurity, greed, anger, contempt, and even hate—prevent deep relationships from flourishing, whether it be among humans, or between a human and his dog. It is the struggle immortal—the yin and the yang. Life doesn't just happen *to* us; it happens *with* us. Our responses to people and events—and yes, a dog—involve our consent. Lashing out, the knee-jerk responses of anger and impatience are always up to us to choose, as are appreciation, understanding, and even joy. Even convincing ourselves that we are justified is a choice. History is littered with examples of great damage done by individuals who felt justified. A simple glance at current domestic and worldwide affairs makes clear this ancient struggle and truth. More important than what happens is our choice about how we respond and act—when slapped upside the head by life or when presented with unexpected joys.

Many walks that I take with Durango Pete happen along ponds, lakes, and rivers. Often, I notice the breeze, however slight it might be, or the landing of an insect so small as to escape my eyes but still be noticeable from the ripples on the water propagated and spread far from that source. Our choices—our behaviors—also create ripples. There is a theory, or a metaphorical concept, coined by Edward Lorenz, called the butterfly effect. This is the idea that small causes can bring about significant changes. The flapping of a butterfly's wings might lead to a change in the path that a tornado would otherwise take.

In *The Vocation of Man*, published in Germany in 1799, Johann Gottlieb Fichte says, "You cannot remove a single grain of sand from its place without thereby…changing something throughout all parts of the immeasurable whole." I would suggest the same is true when we place a grain of sand on a beach—a grain that was not there before.

Perhaps Durango Pete is the grain of sand—or the beating of a butterfly's wings (wild and frantic, I agree)—placed into my life. And for Durango Pete, perhaps, I am the same. A harsh rebuke, a simple stroke of my hand upon his head, changes his day in profound ways. It changes mine too. When he refuses to come, or when he brushes his body against my leg as I sit working in my chair, I am changed in simple and profound ways. Blood pressure rises—or blood pressure falls. I expect that similar responses manifest in him. This very thought process, which I sit here and write, is the result of a little cattle dog named Durango Pete entering my life. I might be engaged in reflection if Pete was not a presence in my world. I am an old man, and it is the common avocation of the elderly to engage in thinking about stuff. But I have no doubts that Durango Pete is the disturbance in my dynamic system that has brought me to this place—the place where I think about the struggles between people, cultures, religions, and a man and a dog and a dog and a man. This book is a reflection of the great change that came about because of him—my return to my roots as a writer.

A dog can teach us a lot—if we open our hearts and minds and put aside our arrogance and desire to be in control. Durango Pete is the gift that brought me to a better place. I like to say, "At the age of five, I was fully connected with my creator—God, if you will. At the age of sixty-six, I am steadily working my way back." Durango Pete is the unlikely vehicle through which this has happened. I had no idea, when I first saw him almost five years ago at an adoption event, how profound our relationship would be, nor what that relationship would allow me to become: a better person. I like to think that Pete feels the same way. I think he does. Perhaps you are on a conscious journey too. Perhaps Durango Pete can be a grain of sand—or a butterfly's wings—in your life as he has been in mine.

Pete is over four years old now. We have had quite the adventure getting to where we are. Oh, he still outsmarts me most of the time, and like the first day I saw him, I am still pretty much a sucker for him. But we have ironed out a few understandings over the years, and life is pretty easy with him now—provided Cynthia and I listen to what he has to say. We have shared travel, treats, time, tender moments, tough times, plenty of talks, and quite a few adventures. Pete and I have sat in the wild places, and we have thought about a lot of stuff. Once in a while, Pete shares a philosophical observation with me. Sometimes, the epiphany about life is mine. Sometimes poetry happens—usually a collaboration of an unlikely sort, you know, a 'mixed-species' Rogers and Hammerstein.

Early on, Pete and I decided to write this book. We aren't done rambling and writing yet, even though I am getting a bit old and creaky. This is a collection of our stories about life, and poetry with a cattle dog philosofur—Durango L. Pete—and me, an old man and his friend.

PART ONE

AT THE BEGINNING

CHAPTER 1

MEET AND GREET – DURANGO PETE

A S FATE WOULD HAVE IT, there were three cattle dogs playing on the floor. They were the remaining siblings of four that had been available originally. One male had already been adopted. Two of the three were red and tan in color. I hardly noticed them. My eyes were immediately drawn to the one who was off-white, with chocolate-brown spots and chocolate-brown ears. He also had a brown eye patch with a caramel-colored spot below the patch. To top it off, he had caramel-colored spots mixed in with the brown spots on his legs. His eyes were a striking amber color—like a wolf or coyote.

It had been two years since I had held a dog that was mine. Now my wife, Cynthia, and I were—after a long time without a pet—considering adopting a rescue dog. We had driven from our home in southwest Denver to an adoption event at a Petco near my childhood home in metro Denver. The event was put on by Colorado Puppy Rescue. Our daughter Krista had prodded us to go. We had planned on looking at a small terrier-mix, but he had already been adopted by the time we arrived. Only a few dogs remained: several black Labs and large mixed-breeds and a partial litter of cattle dogs, one with unique markings like cookies and cream and who had a certain indescribable something about him.

I picked him up, and he licked me like I was his long-lost best friend. He licked my hands, my arms, my neck, and my nose, and he nibbled on my chin whiskers. He was so happy! I turned to my wife and said, "What do you think? Should we do it?"

She said, "Whatever you think, dear."

Was meeting Durango Pete meant to be? I admit that I am a believer in fate, in the concept that major events in our lives do not happen by accident. Two years before, our beloved family dog of eighteen years, Pumpkin Lou, passed away. My wife, Cynthia, and I decided that we were not ready to rescue another dog right away. We needed time to mourn Pumpkin. We sprinkled some of Pumpkin's ashes by the garden window of our home in Mission, Kansas. We spread some more ashes at her favorite park near our house. The rest of her cremains we kept in a small silk purse (she was not a large dog) tied closed with a ribbon of red, and we kept it in the glove box of our car. I know—that sounds a bit freaky. But Pumpkin loved to ride in the car. We knew that the rest of her ashes would one day, when the time was right, be spread high above timberline on Byers Peak near Winter Park, Colorado. For the time being, the glove box and car rides would have to suffice.

After much hard work and time (grief cannot be rushed), and the selling of our house in Kansas and relocating to Colorado, Cynthia and I began to miss the company of a dog, and we began to discuss the idea of adopting a new four-legged family member. Our daughter Krista, who lived close to us in Denver, also encouraged us to get another dog. Daily, I got a text message or an email with a picture of a dog that Krista thought would be perfect for us. They were a variety of breeds, mixed and otherwise, and they were from various shelters and agencies near Denver. I typically responded that the dog was cute, or something along those lines, but that I was not ready to make the move to another dog quite yet. I wanted to take my time. I wanted to throw the idea out to the Universe. I figured that when it was meant to happen, it would. And I figured that the dog that was meant to be with us would be the one who would come along.

The prodding from Krista got Cynthia looking at dogs too. Soon, Cynthia was showing me pictures of dogs she also had located. My usual responses to her suggestions were that the dog had "legs that were too short," or that it was too old, or that I didn't care for its color. Most common of all my responses was that its ears were too long and that they stuck up. I had never owned a stick-up-eared dog. But even though my aversion to dogs with stick-up ears was clear, she kept sending me pictures of dogs with long stick-up ears! My dislike of stick-up ears ended up mattering not a whit. Durango Pete has ears that would make a jackrabbit or mule deer proud.

Somewhere along the line, I had started thinking about a cattle dog for our next pup. I had been introduced to a few of them while we were at our family cabin in Grand Lake, Colorado. My ancestors, including my grandfather, had been ranchers in Colorado for years. My great-grandfather thrice removed had homesteaded a ranch near Boulder, Colorado, in 1860. His grandsons, in turn, homesteaded the Hinman Ranch near Kremmling, Colorado, in the early 1900s. It had always been a dream of mine to own a ranch one day. So I think the idea of having a herding dog, like a cattle dog, was fitting.

One day in September 2012, Krista showed me a picture of a dog that was up for adoption through Colorado Puppy Rescue. They were having an adoption event that day. The dog was not a cattle dog, but it was very cute. Maybe the dog pictures and adoption messages from Krista and Cynthia were finally wearing me down. I agreed to go look at the dog. The adoption event was to conclude at 2:00 p.m. that afternoon. It was 1:00 p.m. when we headed out in the car—Cynthia, Krista, and me. Despite our late start, I thought we could make it to the event in time. Off we sped to check out the little pup. I will confess that I was excited.

About halfway to our destination, we got into a big traffic jam. Time was ticking away, and it was starting to look like we might not make it before the adoption event closed. I know Denver well, and I listed alternative ways to exit the freeway and get to the event. There were problems with each alternate route, and we were so trapped in the line of cars that there was no way for us to reach an exit where we were. We were going to have to stay put and hope for the best. I thought to myself, "Maybe this isn't meant to be." I was disappointed, though. My excitement at the prospect of having a new dog had been growing. Perhaps this traffic jam was a sign that "our dog" was not at this event.

After barely creeping forward, I turned to Cynthia and said, "Oh well, my dear. I don't think we are going to make it before the event closes. I'm sorry." I was sad that we weren't going to arrive in time. But I figured there would always be other events and other dogs to see down the road.

I like to think now that Durango Pete somehow intervened on his and our behalf—that he used his ancient powers and connections with the source to part the cars because, finally, traffic thinned out and we decided to go ahead to the adoption event even though we would just make it before the advertised closing time. We rolled into the pet store parking lot at 1:45 p.m. There were fifteen minutes left until the adoption closed. We made a mad dash inside and found the puppies that remained, but alas, the dog I had wanted to see had been adopted. Seven or eight dogs remained who had not been placed, so we decided to look them over. They included a small group of tiny cattle dogs. Instinctively, I picked up the chocolate-and-cream-colored one.

"Whatever you think, dear." Cynthia had given me her blessing. I looked back down at the tiny fur-puff in my arms. His chocolate ears were folded over in cute fashion as he snuggled in the crook of my elbow. I knew it was a done deal. We had found our dog. Sometimes perseverance, even in Denver traffic, pays off.

The information we received about Durango Pete was minimal. He was dog number 740. He came to Colorado Puppy Rescue through a transfer agency in New Mexico.

They had rescued him from a "kill" shelter. He had been fostered for a short time when he arrived in Denver. Cynthia and I were given a brief note from the foster home where Pete had lived for a short while. The note just said that he was a "sweet dog who loved to give kisses and licks." The kisses and licks I could confirm. The sweet dog part remained to be seen.

Of course, I thought it was cool that he was a cowboy dog from New Mexico since I was from western cowboy stock myself. I did wonder about his background. The thought that he might be a reservation dog crossed my mind. There are a staggering number of strays on the reservations in New Mexico. I did not think about the possibility that he might have been the offspring of a feral dog. Pete's wolf-like eyes certainly made an impression on me, and I knew that feral dogs were wild and presented unique challenges as pets. Instinctively, I wondered how much of a handful this little puppy might prove to be. We were busy with our new little friend and the adoption process. So much information was spinning around in our heads that we didn't spend too much time thinking about his New Mexico background. Fortunately, we did pick up a book about Australian cattle dogs and a book on puppy training before we left the pet store. It had been a long time since I had had a puppy. When I finally got around to reading the book, the information about cattle dog personalities and behaviors would prove to be enlightening—and frightening.

Krista was excited about our decision to adopt one of the cattle dogs. Her lobbying efforts had paid off. Krista nearly left with one of the two remaining sisters. But her dog, Cyrus, was getting old and had lots of health issues. He needed to be the focus of her attention and the star of her household for the time being. The other cattle dog puppies would be adopted at a later event.

We had given most of our dog supplies away or donated them after Pumpkin had passed away. We were not equipped for a new doggy. Shopping began immediately. Cynthia took our new puppy and worked on completing the adoption paperwork and paying the necessary adoption fees. Krista and I grabbed a buggy and started off on a mad dash through the store. We picked up a metal kennel and a portable dog crate. We picked out ten or fifteen different dog toys. We selected a nice doggie bed, a collar, a harness, two leashes, two small bowls for food and water, dog treats, puppy food—dry and canned—and nice shearling pads for his kennel and crate. No one said dog adoption and ownership was cheap!

Eight hundred dollars later we were ready to head home with our new little buddy. We put his handsome little blue collar on him, hooked up his matching leash, and headed for the door. "What is his name?" Cynthia asked me.

"Durango," I responded without hesitation. I had an affinity for the mountain town in the southwest corner of Colorado. We had been to Durango not long before. It had been the final overnight stop on a Wyoming-to-New Mexico bike ride I had done. Plus, the town of Durango was close to New Mexico, and the town certainly had a New Mexico vibe. I figured that some recognition of our new puppy's roots would be appropriate in the naming process. I looked at Cynthia for a response. There was no thoughtful pondering of my suggestion, hand to chin. At the same time, she didn't break out into laughter either. I took both as encouraging signs.

"Pete!" she said firmly.

"Pete?" I replied quizzically. "Why Pete?"

"It just popped into my head," she said. "I think he told me that was his name."

I am not one to downplay another person's epiphanies or insights—especially not my wife's. Plus, I thought Pete was a fine cowboy name and entirely fitting for a cattle dog. I liked the way it rolled off of my tongue. It was as special a name as the dog who had just entered our lives.

"Durango Pete! That's perfect!" I replied with enthusiasm.

So it was that Durango Pete became his name. His southwestern roots had been recognized. Durango was a fine western town with many working ranches nearby. That pleased my ranching sensitivities. Pete was a good old cowboy, Colorado sort of name. All the humans present agreed. I hoped that Pete would wear his name proudly and do justice to such a glorious handle. Durango Pete seemed not to mind the moniker. He was ready to head out of the store, on his first big adventure in Colorado, and take his first short walk to the car—or maybe not.

It is an easy assumption to make—that every dog wants to walk, especially a *cattle dog*! I certainly understood that a leash might not be the favorite thing to experience for a puppy eight to ten weeks old. But Durango Pete went into an immediate pose of frozen puppy dog, seemingly saying, "I ain't going anywhere with this thing around my neck!" There was no budging him. There was no coaxing him. No amount of pleading, prodding, or promise of treats mattered. Pete was firmly planted! I experienced an immediate sense of foreboding—foreshadowing, if you will. Was this an early indication of a stubborn streak? Was this the foot upon which we were to begin this relationship and journey? "Oh my," I thought.

We finally reached the car—after a bit of dragging Pete along and repeated episodes of lifting him up into our arms, reassuring him with kisses and scritches on his head and ears, and placing him back down again in the hope that he would place one tiny paw in front of the other for at least a step or two. Nope. Nonetheless, we persisted, and we eventually reached the car. We should have parked closer.

I am a hopeful man by nature, and I am not one to spend time giving power to negative thoughts or to cower in the face of a challenge. I did, however, wonder about this little dog. As it turned out, this was to be a taste of what would prove to be our first of many big battles with Durango Pete involving leash walking, and it was a prelude to the realization that we were not in for a cakewalk with our little cow dog buddy.

The car ride home with Pete went smoothly. He curled up in my lap and in the crook of my elbow, and he slept the entire ride home. His sleeping in the car was encouraging since we like to travel from Denver up to our family cabin in Grand Lake. We knew that car trips and travel would be common.

We immediately busied ourselves with setting up the house for a new puppy. We put his bed near the gas fireplace for warmth. We put the new toys we had purchased in a container next to his bed. We set up his feeding and drinking stations in the kitchen. Finally, we set up his kennel in our bedroom and put his shearling pad and some old towels and linens inside to make it more comfortable. Durango Pete, in turn, set about exploring every nook and cranny of his new house. We introduced him to his big backyard. But we had to carry him up and down the steps from the deck to the yard. His legs were too short to climb the stairs. He appeared to like his new digs. We set up our schedule to make sure eyes were on him all the time. Puppy potty training had begun.

Pete was mellow for the first few days. But with each passing day and with new experiences, his true personality emerged. We were not prepared for the level of chewing and biting we experienced. Feet, socks, hands, ears, hair, pants legs—all were fair game for his razor-sharp puppy teeth. We also discovered that Durango Pete had sharp claws and that he had a unique ability to use his toes like fingers. He spread his toes outward and then used them to grip with his nails, like an eagle's talons. Wounds to my hands and forearms began to accumulate.

Each evening at 7 p.m., the precise time we were quite worn out from our own work and that of taking care of our new dog, Pete would begin his final, and most severe, case of craziness. His pupils would dilate until his eyes were fully black, like a shark's eyes. He would attack us using teeth and claws. He would jump onto and off the furniture. He would run full-speed through the house, circling around and around and around. Nothing short of physical restraint could stop him, and that wasn't easy. We decided to put him in time-out in his kennel (which we named his "shark cage") to allow him to self-calm. When he was successful, we let him rejoin us unencumbered. Getting Pete into his kennel was no easy task. As soon as he saw it, he attacked it, nipping at it, grabbing it with his teeth, and barking at it as if it were a calf needing to be herded. The nightly routine became known as "shark cage roundup."

As Pete's craziness escalated, and out of our growing concerns about this dog we had brought into our home, we finally picked up our Australian cattle dog book, and we began to do a bit of research in the hope of better understanding him and learning about how to deal with his wild behaviors. The more we read and researched Pete's breed, the more sobering our decision to adopt a cattle dog became. A bit of cattle dog history might be in order.

CHAPTER 2

Durango Pete's Ancestors

THE FIRST THING TO KNOW, and perhaps the most important, is that cattle dogs originated from breeders crossing traditional British herding dogs with the dingo (wild dog) in Australia. In the late 1700s, British citizens began to migrate to Australia. Many of them took livestock and their herding dogs along. These early settlers, farmers, and ranchers soon learned that their traditional British herding dogs were not well suited for life in Australia. The land was far more rugged than their homeland had been, and the distances being ranched and farmed were much greater than in Britain. This vast landscape encouraged the early ranchers to develop very large herds of sheep and cattle. These herds roamed the Australian outback, largely without close supervision. The herds developed some characteristics that were inherent in such a wild and rugged landscape, and they became more unpredictable and wild than more traditional cattle and sheep. The ranchers' traditional sheepdogs were ill-equipped to deal with these new circumstances. The ranchers began to search for a solution and contemplated using cross breeding to develop a new dog that would be better suited to the vast Australian ranches. This is where the dingo first becomes part of this story.

The dingo existed in Australia long before the first white settlers began to appear. The Aboriginal peoples called the wolf-like animal "warragal." Dingo DNA and carbon dating first place the dingo on the Australian continent 3,450 years back. For context, Aboriginal peoples have been in Australia forty thousand to fifty thousand years. The dingo is related to the Indian wolf. It may be that the dingos' domesticated ancestors migrated from India, through Malaysia, to Australia four thousand years ago and that they were used for trade and bartering along the way.

The dingo is distinguished by a separate scientific classification from the traditional domesticated dog, which is derived from the northern timber wolf. The dingo is classified as *canis familiaris dingo*. The early dingos lived independently from aboriginal peoples. But they lived close to Aboriginal families. The dingo lived both in the wild and in the camps at times. Aboriginal peoples took dingo pups from their mothers before the pups' eyes were open. They hand-fed the pups, which resulted in a gradual socialization of the selected dingos. Eventually, the socialized dingos were used for tracking and hunting.

Dingos were important animals in Aboriginal mythology. They were central to The Dreaming, stories of creation. Dingos were believed to live in both the real and mystical worlds. Aboriginal peoples believed that dingos could detect evil spirits and evil people. As such, dingos were important in protecting the Aboriginal communities and their camps. Some stories involve dingos as shape-shifters, able to go from canine to man, man to canine, and some were believed to exist as hybrids. Dingos were important enough to the Aboriginal peoples of Australia that they often named dingos and slept with them, and were sometimes buried with them.

Early accounts of dingos described them as mostly red in color, with white-tipped tails and white feet. Some white or black dingos were also included in early descriptions. Dingos sometimes live alone, but they usually travel in packs of up to ten. They are opportunistic hunters by nature, and they feed on what small and larger game is available. They communicate in a fashion similar to more familiar canines such as wolves—by howling. Pure dingos are becoming rarer in the outback because they will breed with domestic dogs. Dingo behavior is marked, in part, by short periods of high activity followed by rest periods. They are usually most active at dusk and dawn. This is certainly a consistent behavior I see in Durango Pete.

Dingos hunt in packs, and in the wild they usually make the kill by biting the prey's throat. The sheep and cattle that were brought with the early white settlers of Australia soon became new prey for the dingos. The dingos were swift and stealthy killers of the settlers' stock and did not typically bark when on the attack. Dingos often attacked the sheep from behind, biting the sheep's hind legs. Often, enough damage was done from the attack on the legs that the sheep died simply from those wounds. The early European settlers developed a dislike of the dingos because of the damage they inflicted upon their flocks of sheep and their herds of cattle.

Their ability to survive in the harsh outback meant that they were hardy and had evolved to become highly intelligent. Attempts by the early settlers and ranchers to eliminate the dingo simply resulted in even smarter and more formidable foes. The adaptability and intelligence of the dingo did not escape the awareness of the early settlers, who began to consider the dingo as a potential breeding partner to develop a herding dog better suited to the conditions in Australia.

There is ongoing debate over which breeds were utilized in combination with the dingo. In reality, many different breeds were tried over the years. The original sheepdogs used by the early Australian settlers for herding were called Smithfields. Smithfields were heavy dogs with thick black coats, floppy ears, and white markings. Their coat and size were handicaps in the hot Australian landscape and for the distances their new home required they travel while doing their jobs. Additionally, the Smithfields' bite was considered too severe, and they were noisy when herding. A man by the name of Timmins decided to try breeding a Smithfield with an Australian dingo. The resulting dog was a quieter worker but had a severe bite as well. The new dogs could not be trusted around the calves. They became known as "Timmins Biters."

The next significant development in the breeding of the cattle dog is attributed to Thomas Hall of Muswellbrook, New South Wales, in 1840. Hall imported several Blue Smooth Highland Collies. They were blue merle dogs and similar to today's border collies and bearded collies. The offspring of the Highland Collies were bred with the dingo. The dog that resulted was either blue or red speckled. They were known as "Hall's Heelers." These dogs herded livestock by silently sneaking up behind the stock and nipping at the animals' heels. His dogs would immediately lay flat to avoid a nasty kick from the livestock. A man by the name of Thomas Bentley had one of Hall's strains of dogs. This dog was unusually fine, and it had a white mark on his forehead. This dog was only known as "Bentley's dog." Bentley's dog was used to sire other dogs. The hallmark white blaze is commonly seen on contemporary cattle dogs and is called the "Bentley Mark." Durango Pete sports just such a white blaze on his forehead. There is great talk among cattle dog owners today about whether or not the fur of the Bentley Marks is softer than the other fur on the dogs' heads. We haven't decided, although we are leaning toward the "softer" camp.

It was about this time—1840 to 1850—that other breeds that had been crossed with the Hall's Heelers (also called Queensland Heelers), were used. One of the additional breeds crossed with Hall's dogs was the bull terrier. The bull terrier was known for its tenacity, and it was thought that the tenacity characteristic might be valuable for work in the Sydney stockyards. The experiment was discontinued because the resulting dogs were so tenacious that they harmed the cattle. Sometimes I swear I see bull terrier in Durango Pete. His stance, when alert, is very similar to that of a bull terrier, and Pete is as stubborn as a bull.

The dalmatian was also bred with Hall's dogs because of the dalmatian's skills around horses and its loyalty to its owners. Modern cattle dogs are known for their attachment to their people. Durango Pete is starting to demonstrate that he thinks we are OK after all. The story is still unfolding. We shall see if he decides to keep us.

The Kelpie, another breed under development at the time, was the last breed to be utilized in the development of the cattle dog. The Kelpie has many personality and work characteristics similar to the cattle dog, and the Kelpie was developed for the same purpose of working livestock. Durango Pete's ears look very "Kelpie" to me, and his coat and eye color hint at strong Kelpie influences.

The final noteworthy development in the modern cattle dog was a reinfusion of dingo blood around 1940. Some breeders thought that the cattle dog was getting too soft and losing some of the qualities that the dingo had brought to bear. I might have to hold the folks who did this accountable for Durango Pete's hard-nosed craziness.

Of course, we knew none of this information about cattle dogs when we made the spur-of-the-moment decision to adopt Durango Pete. We acquired all this knowledge after the fact and out of desperation to better understand the wild puppy dog that we had brought home. We not only learned the history of the cattle dog, but we also did loads of research about the characteristics and needs of cattle dogs. This information only served to increase our anxiety even more.

Cattle dogs are bred to be working dogs. They need lots of exercise. A fifteen-minute walk around the neighborhood helps, but it is not nearly enough. If a cattle dog does not get enough exercise, it will find a way to entertain itself and get its own exercise. This usually happens with disastrous results. Cattle dogs are extremely intelligent. They are on the list of the ten most intelligent dog breeds. Physical exercise is not enough—they need mental stimulation as well. Oh, they enjoy a good game of tug-of-war, for sure. But they need to be challenged well beyond the typical domestic dog games and activities. When you are sixty-two years old and have a brand-new cattle dog puppy, the exercise demands and the mental stimulation needs of a dog like Durango Pete can be—well—daunting. It has been said by some dog owners that their dog is always one step ahead of them. Cattle dog owners say that cattle dogs are three steps ahead. Cattle dogs deserve much more than to be put in a backyard or in a dog run outside and left to fend for themselves. They are known to be great companions, but only if their owners are willing to invest significant amounts of time, energy, and creativity working with them. When Durango Pete arrived on our scene, I came out of my retirement and became a full-time dog trainer.

Cattle dogs typically weigh twenty-five to fifty pounds as adults. Durango Pete is right in the middle of the scale, at thirty-eight pounds, and that is a good thing. He is incredibly strong, and his smaller size helps me control him when the need arises. Cattle dogs have a reputation for being very stubborn. A good deal of effort is spent early on fighting the battle to establish who is going to be the boss. The cattle dog's wild dingo heritage means the owner needs to be a very strong pack leader or the dog will run roughshod over him. Remember, these dogs were bred to boss around a wild steer, so they had to be strong and tough. Although a cattle dog is not a big dog, it makes up for its smaller size with tenacity, aggression, and confidence. I had quite a job ahead of me.

All this information caused us some concern. Were we up to the task? Most of the training was going to be my responsibility. I wasn't sure that I had the energy to do an adequate job. Plus, it meant that a lot of the activities my wife and I enjoyed doing, and much of the freedom and flexibility we had in our lives, was going to end for the time being. We realized that if we had known about the demands on the owners in raising a cattle dog puppy, we probably would have looked at other breeds or even considered fostering an older dog in need. But we already had signed the adoption papers, paid the fees, and brought Durango Pete home.

I thought back to the signing of Pete's adoption papers with Colorado Puppy Rescue. Most adoption agencies do background checks to ensure that the adopting family has adequate space, resources, experience, and commitment to the dog it is taking with it. I remember recognizing that what we were doing was not a small thing. I certainly had butterflies in my stomach as we completed the paperwork and gathered supplies for Durango Pete. Cynthia and I were no longer youngsters (although Cynthia is well-preserved), and we had been footloose and fancy-free for two years. We had come and gone as we pleased. Travel had been easy. Dining out had been common. But we both realized that something was missing in our house and in our lives. It was true that some of our best years, and our best times, had been those in which our dog, Pumpkin, and our cat, Rocky, roamed our house in Mission, Kansas. And it was true that we missed the joys and heartbreaks that had gathered in our hearts through the simple act of sharing our lives with them and theirs with us.

As Cynthia and I stood there in Petco, Durango Pete in my arms, we decided that we had to make the effort. I realized the seriousness of the commitment we would be making. We had a responsibility to the adoption agency. We had a responsibility to Pete's foster family. We had a responsibility to Under My Wing, the transfer agency in New Mexico to which Pete had been relinquished. We had a responsibility to Pete's original owners, who gave him up. We had a responsibility to Pete's biological parents and his siblings. We had a responsibility to our own Creator, who gives us the free will to be loving or to be fickle and shallow. We had a responsibility to see that Durango Pete would become a vital part of our lives and family and that he would be given that which he needed to become successful and the best dog that he could be. We had a responsibility to ourselves—to honor our humanity.

It was no small thing, the adventure upon which we were about to embark. It was a joyful time. But adopting Pete was also a serious undertaking. We decided that we were going to take it a day at a time and see where that would take us. It is hard, though—to live in the now, in the present moment. We all have expectations. They are filtered through similar experiences in our pasts. They are impacted by our personal histories and the convenient fictions we are prone to create. I had been a three-dog man. The three dogs that had been part of my family over the years impacted my vision for Durango Pete. My love of my ancestors' cattle-ranching heritage and my desire for a working dog helped me to create my own fiction and fantasy of having a cattle dog partner. These filters would play out over the months that my story—our story—with Durango Pete would unfold. Thus it was that we started our big adventure with Durango Pete, a small cattle dog with a big heart and a big attitude.

CHAPTER 3

A SHORT HONEYMOON ENDS

WE HAD A VERY SHORT puppy honeymoon with Durango Pete. We had some good times and some encouraging times for the first few weeks after we brought him home. He was still a bit overwhelmed by the new circumstances in which he found himself. He wanted to be close to us for the first few weeks, and he seemed to enjoy lying in our laps.

One fine fall day, not long after Pete came home with us from Petco, the morning was given birth with a quality of light the softness of which is only perceived during a short span of days in early spring and again in late fall. Surely it is the angle of the sun, which, being less severe, allows its rays to lie down upon the earth with a gentleness that is compelling and hard to ignore. It was a morning that begged Durango Pete and me to go for a walk.

Pete had been a family member for nearly a month. Walking him on his leash had continued to prove challenging even though we had worked diligently on it from the day we adopted Pete. One of our experiments to deal with the challenge was to buy a harness for him. Cynthia and I speculated that the collar, when a leash was attached, might be uncomfortable or disconcerting for Pete. The new harness was deep red and went nicely with his brown ears and caramel eye patch. I thought he looked dashing in it.

We were having nice fall weather, so we spent a lot of time playing in the backyard, and even enjoying "campouts" around our backyard fire pit at night after the sun had gone down. We thought Pete, being a cowboy dog and all, would enjoy our little campfire hangouts. He seemed to. We wrapped him in a blanket and put him in our laps while we enjoyed his company and some downtime with a glass of wine—or two.

I put the new harness on for his morning walk. He was not at all happy about donning the harness, but he was small enough that I could put him on the kitchen island countertop so he couldn't escape. He fought me like a wildcat. I persisted. After using five or six treats for diversion, and sporting a few new wounds to my forearms, I had managed to get the harness on (it looked quite handsome, I must say). I relocated Pete to the floor. We were ready to head out the door. Hope springs eternal.

Pete had other ideas. He put his chest to the floor, hind end up in the air, and dug in with his four-wheel brakes, refusing to budge. No amount of verbal coaxing helped. Treats were not effective. "What kind of cattle dog does not want to go outside and explore?" I thought to myself.

Was he afraid? Did he not like being with me? Of course, Cynthia was not having any more success walking him than I was. If it was a dislike of us, at least he was not selective. I was frustrated and feeling perplexed—angry even. I knew that Pete needed the exercise and that leash-walking skills were vital to his participation in our family and society. Instinctively, I snatched him up from the floor, and I marched him out of the house in my arms. I put him down outside. Butt up, brakes on, no success. I picked him up again and walked half a block. I put him back down. Butt up! Pete refused to walk. I repeated this drill several more times. Finally, when we were several blocks from the house, he took a few steps. Hallelujah!

I discovered that if I walked with him in my arms two blocks down from our house to the park trail, he would reluctantly do some walking from that point forward. If he stopped, I lifted him up by his harness and marched him forward a few feet and then set him back down. Then he would walk another ten to fifteen feet, and we would do this all over again. So it went. The beautiful fall weather went unnoticed by me. I was fully engaged in work, my mind swirling with thoughts about how to solve this problem, what would happen if he could not learn to leash walk, and for the first time since we had brought him home, the thought of having to relinquish him exploded into my mind. That thought was staggering, and it brought a wave of nausea to my stomach. I had to find a way to help Durango Pete overcome his dislike of the leash.

Of course, Pete took frequent opportunities to sniff this weed or that bush and to bask in the warm sunshine. He seemed wholly unconcerned with my silent desperation, unfazed by the lifting and pulling on his leash, and impervious to my impatient barking of commands to "walk, dammit!" The park and pond trail near our house was about a half a mile in length. It took us an hour to complete the circuit. I was exhausted when we arrived home. Pete seemed to be happy as a clam. Some cattle dog!

About the same time, his biting, chewing, and digging started to emerge and escalate. I will be the first to admit that I am obsessive-compulsive about many things. Our yard and landscaping are among those things. Pete had identified one special spot in the backyard grass, and he began to tunnel his way to China. When we caught him, we scolded him verbally and immediately relocated him. I filled the hole back in with dirt. It became a maddening game. No one won. Clearly, Pete didn't care for my yelling. I didn't care for his inconsiderate digging.

The mulch in the garden along the back fence was his favorite playground, for there resided an infinite supply of chew toys—the larger pieces of brown mulch. Deep holes began to appear in the mulched areas of the gardens, companions to the growing hole in the grass. Once again, scolding (never hitting), relocating him, and providing him with appropriate alternative chew toys were our interventions and shaping responses. We made little progress. And we were concerned about him swallowing pieces of wood.

He pulled the grass out in clumps. He chewed on the low-hanging branches of our lilac bushes. He chewed up the doormat by the sliding door to the deck. We sprinkled the lawn liberally with chew toys and bones—desperate attempts to redirect his chewing to more appropriate targets.

We played ball games in the backyard to engage him in exercise and problem-solving. The ball games were one-sided affairs. He was eager to chase the ball, but he refused to bring it to us after he had it in his mouth, preferring a game of keep-away. I got most of the exercise and did most of the problem-solving. It all seemed backward and bizarre. None of my previous dogs, or my experiences with them, seemed to relate to Durango Pete.

Pants legs, stocking feet, hands, arms, and ears were all irresistible targets for his snapping jaws and needle-sharp teeth. I had scratches and wounds everywhere. Cynthia was reluctant to play with Pete on the floor. Every transgression was met with a technique meant to shape his behavior and eliminate his frustrating and painful aggression and play. We read even more information about how to deal with these behaviors in cattle dog puppies. I bought more books by experts. I visited site after site online.

Physical techniques or punishment were not recommended by the experts, especially with this breed. We "yelped" or hollered "ouch" when he bit or scratched us. We ignored him by turning our backs or even leaving him, walking away without looking at him. We hoped this would extinguish his attacks. He persisted. We did it again and again.

We redirected him to appropriate chew toys. He had plenty because we kept buying them in a hopeless effort to find one that would engage him and spare us his teeth. Pete knew them by their names. Clearly, this dog was not stupid. He could identify them by request and pick up any of them, including his Orangey, his Kabluey, his Cattle Cow, his Chicken, his Fox Trot, his Monkey Arm, his Leatherette, his Froggie, his Rope a Dope, and his Hoop a Doop. He had assorted tennis balls and two Kongs, and he knew all of his toys by name within the first six weeks he lived with us.

On a more positive note, his potty training was going very well. Of course, eyes were upon him all the time, and ample outside opportunities were provided. When he awakened in the morning or after a nap, outside we took him. After he was done eating or drinking, outside he went. After he was done playing or roughhousing, we took him outside too. If we observed him sniffing or acting funny, outside he would go. We worked with him so that he would learn vital words like "poopee" and "peepee." Three times a night, we awakened and took him outside to do his duty. I learned to appreciate the stars and to listen for the coyotes and even bugling elk when I took him out for his nighttime potty breaks. The thin air in Colorado allows sounds to carry. I am sure even distant neighbors were awakened by the sounds of me saying, "Go poopee, Durango," or "Go peepee, Durango," and "Nice poopee, Durango Pete!"

Other early victories were also won. We began working on tricks daily. Now, I will confess, I had had some success with previous dogs—Pumpkin, Champ, and even our family dog when I was a little boy. His name was Snuffy Smith. So I approached this task with some confidence—despite Pete's craziness.

By now, Pete was developing a palate for certain treats and foods. Pete had developed a special fondness for cheese—cheddar preferably, medium better than mild or sharp, yellow more attractive than white. He had also discovered the joy of hot dogs, certainly not good for humans or dogs, but a desperate man often turns to desperate measures. These treats proved to be effective stimuli and rewards.

Twice each day, fifteen minutes was dedicated to trick training. We had no set times. We did it when Cynthia and I could both participate and when Pete seemed to be in a calmer state.

When Pete had reached the ripe old age of ten weeks, we conducted our first formal trick training session with him. I was prepared for repeated trials being conducted over a week or several weeks for Pete to learn a trick. I was braced for frustration on my part and a short attention span on Pete's. I showed Pete a fine chunk of the yellow cheese. He was standing by the kitchen island—on all fours. He sniffed it up real good, his little brown nostrils wiggling with delight. I said, "Pete, look," holding the cheese up high with my fingertips. He was focused like a laser. Then I combined the next command with my opposite hand held up, palm forward. "Pete, sit!" I said, and I walked toward him with my palm moving in a downward direction. Immediately, he sat. I gave him the cheese, and Cynthia and I showered him with praise. "Good boy, Pete! What a good doggy!" We tried to pat him on the head, providing him a bit of tactile love and reward too. He shook his head away, all the time looking at the hand that had given him the treat. I got the message loud and clear: "Again, Dad!"

We repeated the sit drill five or six times. Every time he nailed it. We moved on to the next trick—the "down" command. I would like to say that it went as easily as sit. It did not. Still, within fifteen repeated trials, using a bit of a push between his shoulder blades and holding the cheese very close to the ground, he mastered the "down" command. We were on a roll! I was giddy. And I was beginning to see a side of Durango Pete that would manifest more and more as the days, weeks, and years with him accumulated. Pete had an intellect that was not to be underestimated.

Within the first few weeks following our first trick training session and his mastery of sit and down, Durango could back up, shake hands, high five, turn around in both directions, stand on his hind legs, feign a shot dog using the command "*bang*" (I know—I am conflicted about this trick too, but it appears to be a common cattle dog trick), and crawl on command. As we continued our daily trick training sessions, I noticed that Pete would often do the trick I had in mind before I moved a hand or said a word. I purposely mixed the tricks up, making sure that he was not simply learning a routine (although that would be impressive in and of itself). He continued to display this mind-reading ability despite any confounding variables I might present. I now know that he usually knows what I am thinking before I know I am thinking it. I have learned to be very careful about the things upon which I am cogitating in Durango Pete's presence.

Even though he had learned many tricks and commands, the leash problems and the lack of improvement with biting and chewing concerned us and were wearing on us. We were taking Durango Pete with us on frequent outings too. We knew the importance of socializing him with new people and dogs and exposing him to new experiences and environments. Cattle dogs are notorious for being wary around strangers if they are not exposed to new people and new environments when they are young.

Durango loved meeting new people, and he loved meeting dogs too. We wanted to encourage these traits.

We started small, taking Pete with us to our local Safeway and sitting outside while Cynthia and I sipped a coffee and a hot tea. We took him to other coffee shops nearby— to provide him with a change of scenery, circumstances, and people. These trips were encouraging. We were making progress.

One beautiful Saturday in late fall, we decided to up the ante. We took him to a farmers market not far from our house. People were out and about in large numbers. Music played from one of the many white-tented booths that dotted the parking lot, and there was a constant hum of voices chatting and laughing as people enjoyed the day. There were children, small and large, and people of all ages. There were dogs—lots of dogs. As we left the car and approached the crowd with Pete in his harness and on his leash, my anxiety began to mount, and I wasn't sure that we had made a good decision to come. I hoped that Pete was not picking up on my discomfort and unease. I am sure that he did.

In contrast to most of his outings on his leash, in this instance Pete was eager to reach the party, which appeared before his eyes. He almost dragged us along. He made a beeline for the bratwurst/sausage booth, which happened to be owned and managed by a high school classmate of mine (fantastic food, by the way). We followed, trying to reel him in. His greeting of my friend was exuberant. His whole body wiggled, and he jumped on her repeatedly to greet her. We tried to control him, pulling on his leash and hollering "off" commands. None of it worked. Then he tried to reach the tables in the booth and a display where some of the sausages were located as customers looked over the goods and perused their purchases. Our wrestling match with him continued. It was time to move on. We thanked my friend, apologized for Pete's undisciplined behavior, and quickly moved away.

Every booth presented an opportunity for Pete to turn in a repeat performance. And he did. Plus, small children were a perfect size to jump on and lick faces, much to the horror of many of the parents. Other dogs offered a chance for a game of around and around until leashes were hopelessly tangled and intertwined and owners tripped and nearly taken down. Enough was enough. I picked Pete up from the ground and placed him in my arms with a death grip. There he remained until we could extricate ourselves from the crowd and safely reach our car. As we hustled along, Pete in my arms, to my amazement I spied a booth advertising dog training. The name of the company seemed prophetic: "Sit Means Sit!" As we scurried by, I reached out and grabbed a business card.

We made it out of the market safely, sausages intact, children contaminated but unharmed, adults horrified by the lack of training and control of our dog we had displayed. Our egos were bruised. Any progress we had made with Pete was forgotten. At this point, I must say, we researched many dog training companies and methods, including the one whose card I had snatched. None of them seemed like a good fit for us. Many of the companies used e-collars (sending a low-level electric shock for getting a dog's attention and to extinguish undesirable behaviors) to shape behavior. Cynthia and I had strong aversions to this method. I was certain that Pete would agree. For the time being, we persisted in our own methods and in our own way. That would change down the road.

When enough time had passed that we had recovered from our outing with Pete to the farmers market, we began to venture out once more. We kept the outings to places we knew were less stimulating for Pete and where we were in friendly company. We still wanted him to get used to other people and, importantly, other dogs. A common outing for us was to take Durango Pete to our daughter's house, which was near ours. Pete knew Krista well. She had her own dog, Cyrus, and we wanted Pete to learn to be around him. The weather was turning colder, but we enjoyed sitting by Krista's fire pit in the late afternoon and even after dark. We wanted Pete to get used to campfires because backpacking and camping were some of our favorite things to do in Colorado. The backyard get-togethers with Krista let Pete acclimate to the fires and to spending time with Cyrus.

Cyrus was a big dog. He looked more like a grizzly bear than a dog. Pete was immediately smitten by Cyrus. He could not contain himself. Maybe Pete thought Cyrus was a big steer. That is exactly the behavior that Durango Pete demonstrated when he was with Cyrus. He was going to herd that big dog come hell or high water. Pete ran behind Cyrus, nipping at his hind legs. He ran under Cyrus, and through his legs. He jumped on Cy's neck and nipped at him there. Cy was a good sport—for a while. When he had had enough, Cy growled, nosed Durango Pete, and with his massive red neck sent Pete flying. Pete simply dusted himself off and back he came, undaunted.

Cy got weary of Pete's pestering after a while and tried to ignore him. When that wasn't successful, Cy resorted to clamping Pete's entire head in his jaws. Pete would squeak, roll to his back, and offer Cy his belly, demonstrating good, submissive behavior. But as soon as Cy released Pete, the herding game began again. Poor Cy. He was infinitely patient. We liked to say that Cy was Durango Pete's Zen master. This play with Cyrus was typical cattle dog behavior, for sure. He might not be good on the leash, but Pete could herd with the best of them. Except the bad news was that there was no end to this behavior. Inevitably, we separated Pete from Cyrus by putting Pete in his kennel, or we put Pete on his leash to control him. Often, when Pete was especially persistent with harassing Cy, we simply had to leave Krista's house and return home.

When Durango Pete was with Cyrus and when Pete's annoying harassment of Cy escalated out of control, verbal commands and physical prompts did not register. It was as if we didn't exist. Pete never felt our hands on him or our voices. It was eye-opening to see. We were used to dog-sitting Cyrus when Krista was traveling out of town for work. We were fond of Cyrus, and he enjoyed coming to our house for sleepovers when Krista was gone for work. That had become impossible. Cyrus had become nervous and miserable around Durango Pete. He was too old to constantly battle our cattle dog. We tried keeping Cy as we had done so often in the past, but it was becoming too stressful for him—and for us as well. Sadly, the visits and sleepovers at our house ended.

The stress of working with Durango Pete was starting to take a toll on me. My day started at 5:30 a.m., when

Pete would stir. We had a short play period on our bed. This always ended badly, me injured from teeth or claws and Durango Pete in the doghouse. I was up by 6:00 to let him outside. Next, he was fed. By 6:30, he was in his dog bed by the fireplace for a short postbreakfast nap, and I did some writing. At about 7:30 or 8:00, he started to look for trouble, usually annoying his mom, who was working from home. Durango Pete attacked her stocking feet, or he stole the slippers from her feet. After the usual interventions were tried—and failed—Pete ended up in jail (his kennel). Back to the shark cage he went, his eyes dark as coal. While he was in the shark cage, I got dressed and gathered up the walking gear. When I had everything ready for our walk, I let him out of the shark cage, put his harness on, and we headed out the door for our walk. By then it was 9:00 a.m. The walks took us an hour at a minimum. We were back at the house by around 10:00. I took him directly to the backyard to let him run free, get his crazies out, and play ball or Frisbee with him. At 10:30, he came in and took a short nap. At 11:00, he awakened and started biting. I quickly rummaged around to find his rope toy, and I got down on the floor to play some tug with him. Tug often ended when he bit me instead of the rope. I yelled, "Ouch!" and then ignored him. We played a few more rounds, working on teaching him that biting me hurt and was not allowed. At 11:30, we spent time working on tricks for fifteen minutes or so, using verbal commands, hand signals, and treats coupled with praise and rubs for rewards and motivation. Lunch took place around 11:45 or noon. Following lunch, Pete slept for an hour or an hour and a half. At 1:30 p.m., he woke up from his nap and got rambunctious again. We either headed back outside to play "cattle ball" (more about that later), or we got down on the floor and played another round of tug. At 2:00, we practiced our tricks with treats again. When 3:00 rolled around, Cynthia finished work. Cynthia took Pete for his afternoon walk, and I hit the shower. From 4:00 to 5:30, we did the best we could. Dinner for Pete was at 5:30. Sometimes he got an additional short walk to the mailbox, or if we were lucky, Krista stopped by and played with Pete for an hour or so. Krista ended up teaching Pete many of his new tricks. Thank God for Krista. By 7:30 to 8:00 we all were in bed—exhausted.

I was really beginning to wonder whether I would be able to maintain the lifestyle that Durango Pete was demanding. Our world had shrunken overnight. We did not feel comfortable taking Pete to the family cabin in Grand Lake. Our own workouts had fallen by the wayside because Pete's needs and exercise had taken priority. Shopping trips or leisurely dinners out had become a thing of the past. I was not sleeping well because I was getting up three times each night to take Durango Pete out to go to the bathroom. Pete was learning tricks fast, but beyond that, progress was slow to nonexistent. He was still terrible on his leash, and his biting was escalating.

One day I had a breakdown. Cynthia was up early and working at her desk in our home office. I gathered our walking gear and left the house for a walk with Durango Pete. The weather was sunny, but it had taken a cold turn. The wind was blowing out of the northwest hard enough to set the water at our local neighborhood pond into motion. The waves were high enough to fold over into whitecaps.

Perhaps it was the cold weather and the strong winds that put Durango Pete into a wild frame of mind. Perhaps it was the dingo in him or his rough New Mexico heritage. I cannot know. He was as crazy as a wildcat.

Nothing went right from the start. He refused to walk. I resorted to lifting him by his harness to get him to make even the slightest forward progress. My back started to ache. I was wearing a waist pack with his treats and poop bags. He started jumping on me, looking for treats. He would not stop. When I refused to buckle under and give him a morsel, he stood back and barked and barked. A cattle dog bark is ear-piercing. Each time I tried to make forward progress, he either refused or he bit the leash, grabbing it in his teeth and shaking it side to side or pulling it in a maddening game of tug-of-war. When I could make progress forward, he grabbed my pants cuffs in his mouth, snarling and ripping the fabric. The short trip around the pond took us nearly two hours. Finally, the coup de grâce occurred. A fellow walker approached us with a dog of his own on a leash. As he passed, and out of the blue, Durango Pete leaped at the dog, growling and barking, pulling on my leash with a strength that far exceeded his small size. I snapped. I jerked the leash and harness and Pete came flying to me. I hollered *"bad dog,"* grabbed him from the ground, and double-timed it back to the house. I spoke not a word more.

When I arrived back home, Cynthia was still seated at her desk hard at work. She looked up as I entered. "Hi, dear. How did the walk go?"

I did not respond to her question. I simply sat Pete down roughly, unhooked his leash, threw my waist pack on the kitchen counter, and said, "I'm leaving! He's all yours." With that, I turned and walked out of the house and drove away.

Cynthia was stunned by my behavior. In twenty years of marriage, she had never seen me like that. It was hard for her to focus on her work after I left. She sat there and stewed about what to do. I have no idea what Durango Pete was thinking. I am sure that he didn't care. That was part of the problem. I had no idea if Pete had any connection or real bond with us—outside of our provision of food and shelter. Cynthia was feeling the same way.

Cynthia was worried about my health. After the incident, she was concerned that Durango Pete's demands and behaviors were impacting my well-being in a damaging way.

The previous year had been very difficult for me. I had suffered a serious mountain bike accident that resulted in seventeen rib fractures, a punctured left lung, and internal bleeding. Not long after the mountain bike accident, I had prostate surgery. There had been some unpleasant complications following that surgery. I was still not feeling like my old self when we adopted Pete. Durango Pete had been with us only a short while. I was exhausted.

Later that evening, after I had returned home, Cynthia and I had a serious discussion about the day's events, our circumstances, and Durango Pete. I said, "Cynthia, I don't know what to do. I don't feel like Pete has any sort of bond with us. Heck, I don't know if he even likes us—or cares." Cynthia agreed. We had never experienced anything like this with previous pets. We were fully down in the dumps. Pete was resting in his kennel but listening to everything we were saying, his stick-up ears visible in the fading light.

As we talked, the option of returning Pete to the adoption agency, or looking at other placement options, was raised. It was previously unimaginable that we would contemplate such a thing. We had expected to be successful. Pete lay there in the dark, listening to all of this.

We agonized over what do. We cried. We were heartbroken at the idea. But we were fully worn out and at our wits' end. We knew that the longer we tried to work with Pete—even if we used outside trainers—the older he would get and, if we were not successful, the harder it would be to place him and rehome him. Cynthia and I spent a restless night.

The following morning, I called the adoption agency, and a representative said that returning Pete was still an available option. I couldn't make that decision on the phone, so I said Cynthia and I would discuss it. In the meantime, Cynthia had contacted a local agency called New Hope Cattle Dog Rescue and Rehoming of Colorado. Cynthia talked with a very kind and knowledgeable lady at the agency about our exhaustion and our doubts about whether we had the energy, tenacity, and patience to be cattle dog puppy owners. She knew exactly what we were talking about. We sent her a picture of Durango Pete to establish that he was a cattle dog. She confirmed from the picture that Pete was surely a cattle dog. She was encouraging about being able to find a new home for Pete. She also gave us the name of a local trainer who specialized in cattle dogs. He had been a resource for the agency for some time. Cynthia thanked her for her kindness and assistance.

We waffled and agonized over what to do. But despite our anguish, we were strongly leaning in the direction of parting with Durango Pete, and we were heartbroken. Our kids, especially Krista, were disappointed to hear that we were possibly giving up Pete. She was devastated. Krista had been with Durango Pete from the first day. She only lived a mile from us, so Krista had spent loads of time with Durango Pete after we brought him home. She had taught him many of the tricks he had learned. But Krista knew we were struggling with Pete's less desirable behaviors. Her brother, Dallas, also knew that we were considering relinquishing Durango Pete. Both lobbied very hard for Pete. Krista was away on business when we called her to say what we were considering. She had to leave work when she heard the news. She was in tears the rest of the day.

Durango Pete had been especially troublesome the day before my meltdown. But that sort of behavior was not unique. Cynthia and I had been dealing with it for weeks. The crises had been developing since we had brought Pete home. We had not abdicated our responsibilities; we had been working diligently with Pete. He was a mystery, a handsome, maddening, wild mystery. That he was smart was clear. That he loved us was not. I wondered what he was thinking—what he had heard and what he knew about that was being considered by us.

The following day, the day after my crisis and the day when we had contacted both agencies about relinquishing Pete, he had a major change in his behavior. Life is fascinating, as are we and the creatures large and small who inhabit this space. Knowing now how smart Pete is, I am sure he knew something was up. We were not ourselves. I had already started to physically distance myself from him in order to make it less difficult to say goodbye. Cynthia was crying a lot. Neither of us could focus on anything. Neither of us wanted to eat. We wandered about in a fog of dark imaginings, guilt, and remorse. That night we went to bed, sure that we would part with him the next day. Pete was in his kennel. Cynthia and I could not sleep. We tossed and turned. We lay there in the darkness staring at the ceiling, each of us in our own turmoil. Finally, after hours of silence, we turned toward each other. We embraced, and then we started talking about our decision.

By now, Cynthia and I had moved well down the mental and emotional path of letting Durango Pete go. A certain numbness and resignation had set it. But as we talked, the pain of losing Pete was clearly still there.

Pete was quiet in his kennel. Life is full of surprises and ironies. Despite all that had taken place, despite our aloofness with Durango Pete at the time, he had been a good boy all day. There was something in the air about him that had taken a turn. Cynthia and I talked about it. Cynthia tossed out the idea of contacting the recommended trainer and seeing what he thought about Pete's behaviors and training. She talked about giving Durango Pete a second chance. I didn't respond immediately. I turned it all over in my head again and again.

What if nothing changed? What if I simply got angrier and angrier with Pete? I didn't like how I was beginning to feel—or be. I had no idea what I was going to say.

Pete looked at me in the darkness from his kennel. Who was this dog?

CHAPTER 4

TIM THE TRAINER:
THE ALPHA ROLL AND SERIOUS TRAINING BEGINS

LATER THAT NIGHT, THE NIGHT when Cynthia and I tossed and turned, the night when she asked me to give Pete another chance, the night when Pete sat alone in his kennel looking at us, I finally replied to Cynthia.

My reply came from somewhere deep. It was not a cerebral response. It was from my gut and from my heart. I held Cynthia close, and I said, "I am willing to give it a go. I think we should try the trainer and see what happens."

I was willing to give it another couple of weeks. Cynthia was relieved. I was unsure whether I was relieved or not. Perhaps Pete was relieved. We looked over at his kennel. There he sat, on his haunches, sidesaddle-style, as he is known to do. His ears were fully erect. His pale coat glowed in the moonlight that now streamed through our bedroom window. "Pete! Looks like you have another shot at this, buddy," I said. "I hope you make the best of it!"

Cynthia got out of bed and opened the kennel. She carried Pete up and into bed with us. He was overjoyed to be out of the shark cage. He wiggled and wriggled and licked us all over. But he never bit us or scratched us with his claws. We rubbed him up and scritched him behind his ears plenty. Tears streamed down both of our faces. Pete settled down between us, and he slept the whole night through, in our bed—the first time he had ever done that.

The next day, Krista and our other two kids got the news about Durango's pardon. They were beyond relieved—and they were happy. As for Cynthia and me? We were relieved on the one hand. And we experienced trepidation on the other. Pete? He arose and ate a hearty breakfast.

Cynthia and I had exactly zero experience with dog trainers. My mom had done most of the training of Snuffy Smith, my childhood dog. My first wife and I had trained Champ, our Yorkshire terrier. Cynthia and I had rescued our previous dog, Pumpkin, when Pumpkin was a year old. Much training had already been done with Pumpkin by her original owner. What remained to be done in training Pumpkin was handled by me—with Cynthia's help. Neither of us had ever used a professional dog trainer.

I had watched Cesar Milan and another dog trainer on television. A lot of what Cesar did in training his dogs made sense to me. However, some of his tactics seemed harsh. I was hoping that in our training of Durango Pete, and in our relationship with Durango Pete, we could avoid some of the harsher training. Pumpkin had certainly spoiled us. She was, as we liked to say, "one hundred pounds of a bundle of pure love," even though she only weighed seventeen pounds. We had been hoping for things to proceed with

Pete in a similar fashion. Of course, that expectation or hope had already been dashed. Durango Pete was all cattle dog. He had a big attitude wrapped up in a small but strong package.

We had dabbled with using a clicker, but it really did not seem any more effective than the more traditional approaches that I had used with Champ and Pumpkin. The traditional technique of command—vocal paired with hand signals and rewards through the immediate provision of a treat and praise—had been adequate with Champ and Pumpkin. Repeated trials over days and weeks had resulted eventually in success. I had never used clicker training with any of my other dogs.

The traditional methods we were using had led to some successes, as I have mentioned. Pete would now consistently sit on command. "Down" was consistently done provided Pete knew you had a treat in your hand. "Stay" was progressing nicely too. "Come" was very spotty. In the house, with few distractions, Pete was consistent. Outside, especially if he was distracted, which was usually the case, he was inconsistent to poor about responding to a "come" command. This was of great concern to us because we envisioned Pete being off his leash with us on backpacking trips. For his safety, he needed to come when we requested.

Our main concerns to discuss with the trainer were Pete's poor leash behavior, his difficulty in coming to us consistently on command, his biting and herding behaviors, and the fact that he did not seem all that connected to us. We were really concerned that Pete did not appear to love us the way that Pumpkin had. I could see that there was still a big battle going on between Pete and us (especially me) about who was going to be the head honcho of our little rodeo.

We contacted the trainer who had been recommended by New Hope Cattle Dog Rescue and Rehoming of Colorado. His name was Tim. Cynthia set up an appointment for him to come to our house and meet Durango Pete. Tim told Cynthia that he would be bringing along one of his dogs, a cattle dog named Zippy. He wanted to see how Pete behaved around another dog. He also reminded us that puppies learn from their mothers. Pete had been separated from his mom and siblings at seven weeks or earlier, possibly as early as five or six weeks. Pete had missed out on some family learning from his mom and siblings, and Tim thought Zippy might help in teaching Pete appropriate behaviors.

At the appointed day and time, Tim rolled up in his pickup truck. The paint was faded and patchy in spots, and the truck sported a fair share of pockmarks, dents, and scratches. When he finally parked in front of our house, the truck settled into a slightly lopsided angle of repose. We could see a dog face peering out through the window. The markings were dark and consistent with those of a blue heeler cattle dog. The ears were straight up at full attention. Yep—a cattle dog!

Tim opened the door, stiffly unfolded himself from the driver's seat, and reached for the ground with a faded, scuffed boot in tan leather. He wasn't an old man, but he was no youngster either. He was six feet tall, bowlegged, and on the lean side except for a bit of a paunch around the midsection. Red hair sprouted everywhere from beneath his ball cap, which had clearly been with him a very long time and had seen many dog training sessions. He left Zippy in the truck.

Tim shuffled his way across the street to where Cynthia and I awaited. Durango Pete was behind the glass at the front door, checking out the situation. Tim reached us after a bit, and he put his weathered hand out. "Hello there. I'm Tim—Tim, the trainer sent by New Hope." I took his hand, and we had a good manly sort of shake and greeting. He tipped his hat at Cynthia. "Good afternoon, ma'am," he said in a voice smooth but with a hint of country. Cynthia greeted him in return.

"OK, where's this dog, Durango Pete? I guess now's as good a time as any to meet him."

Tim, it turned out, was quite a character. He grew up in Colorado, but spent a great deal of time in Wyoming working on various ranches. Tim had met a lot of cattle dogs during his years spent in Wyoming. Tim loved Wyoming, but he told us he had to leave before "he started to get weird." Wyoming is full of characters and unique sorts of chaps and chappettes. Tim looked like a Wyoming ranch hand. He was ropey and well ripened by the sun. His longish, strawberry blond hair, a few days' growth of facial hair, and "I ain't in a hurry" way of moving served to confirm his Wyoming cowboy ways.

Now, I have already said that I am a big believer in the idea that much of what happens to us in life is not happenstance or coincidence. I believe in fate and the idea that certain people and connections in our lives appear and reappear. As I was having a casual conversation with Tim, I discovered that he was the older brother of a student I had taught at Belmont Junior High School in Edgewater, Colorado, many years before. She had been a favorite student of mine in the language arts class I taught. Her name was Gina. In fact, I had named my first daughter after her. Here, Gina's brother stood before me—the man to whom we were looking for help in saving Durango Pete and us. Maybe working with Tim was meant to be, and the Universe had provided him.

Durango Pete immediately connected with Tim. Tim carried a big pouch of treats on his waist. Tim used clicker training along with treat rewards for rewarding and encouraging appropriate behavior from Pete. Pete is a chowhound, for sure, and a waist pouch full of treats certainly drew Pete's attention to Tim. More than that, though, Tim has a magical touch with dogs. He is calm, deliberate, firm, and patient. Watching Tim greet Pete and start connecting and working with our crazy dog, we were impressed and hoped that Tim would prove to be a "cattle dog whisperer."

Tim was impressed with Durango's focus when given commands to sit, touch, turn around, and come. Tim had let Zippy out of the truck to see Pete's response to an older cattle dog. Tim thought that Durango displayed appropriate responses around Zippy. Pete was just as excited to play with Zippy as he was when he was around Cyrus. When Zippy had enough of Pete's jumping on him and nipping at Zip's heels, he let Pete know with a growl and bared teeth. Pete immediately went to his back, giving up his belly to Zippy. Tim was also watching Pete's tail position and his postures and felt that he was seeing appropriate displays from Pete.

After the first bit of training, Zippy found a shade tree and lay down. Tim talked to us at length about cattle dog personalities and the importance of exercise and mental challenges for them. He got down on a knee in the grass, with Pete on his leash next to him. Tim looked up at us and said, "Here's the thing, you guys. And you gotta remember this. Cattle dogs were bred to be tough. They were bred to be stubborn. And their herding dog genes and dingo heredity means they are damn smart. When you are in the middle of a herd of ornery cattle and you are trying to do your job—getting the strays to go where they need to be—ya gotta be smart and stubborn. When one of the big beasts kicks you in the head, ya gotta be tough." He gave Pete a scratch on the head and then continued his talking. "Cattle dogs are not a breed for the lazy," he said. "You have to be as smart as they are—or smarter. You have to be as stubborn as they are—or more so. You have to be as creative as they are—or better." Finally, he told us, "Listen, guys. If you are willing to put in the time and energy—if you are willing to stay the course—I will tell you that this here is a good dog. There is something about him—maybe it's the eyes? I don't know. He's a bit scary smart. Maybe he's part wolf or coyote? I don't know what it is, but I think he's worth the effort."

Cynthia and I didn't interrupt. Everything Tim had said registered with us. We had seen all of the things he was describing. Once again, my anxiety started to rise. I could feel the familiar tightening in my chest and the swirling of butterflies in my gut, but at least we had boots on the ground. Hopefully, with Tim, Pete and Cynthia and I could make some new headway and progress. Cynthia and I were all ears as Tim continued to talk about cattle dogs and training.

"Here's the thing, you guys. Cattle dogs are stubborn, and they will challenge their owners for dominance," he said. "I spent some time training with Cesar Milan in California. I liked a lot of the stuff—techniques he used—for training. But I like to do my own thing. So I take the stuff that he used—that I liked and that seemed to work for me. But there are a few things that I think are debatable and just don't sit real well with who I am and what I think."

We waited to hear what Tim didn't like.

"I'm gonna show you a technique that Cesar and some trainers use. Now, I know how to do it. And I'd be a liar if I said that I have never done this technique with certain dogs. But I don't use it any more. It makes me feel bad—and I think it injures a dog's psyche."

We waited, impatient to hear what this controversial technique was.

"It's called the alpha roll," Tim said. "Some experts think that, because dogs were domesticated from wolves and because they think a wolf will do this technique in the pack to establish dominance, the alpha roll is a proper tool to use so that a dog owner can establish himself or herself as the alpha dog—the pack leader."

Cynthia and I had, in fact, seen this technique used on the television shows we had watched about dog training. It is also true that I never liked it. There was something about it that I found disturbing on an instinctual level.

The alpha roll is meant to replicate a technique alleged to be used by wolves. Belief in this technique was derived from a study done in the 1940s, which is now believed to have had many flaws. Among them: the space in which the wolves lived was too small and did not replicate conditions experienced by wolves in the wild; the wolves used did not represent an appropriate mix of animals who would make up a pack in the wild; the study was short-term and looked at a very small part of wolf behavior and then extrapolated that to generalizations about wolf behavior; and finally, conclusions were made about wolf-dog, dog-dog, and dog-human behaviors and interactions that were not based on fact.

The alpha roll remains controversial. Most animal behaviorists and trainers do not believe the technique is appropriate. Most believe that it is not the alpha dog that forces this behavior by using a rough technique, but that the giving up of the belly is initiated by the submissive dog voluntarily. It is an "appeasement ritual."

Tim continued to stress the fact that he was not an eager proponent of the technique. He felt it was not needed in most cases and was not only potentially harmful to the dog's psyche but also damaging to the relationship between the owner and the dog.

"Now, I'm going to show you guys how the roll is done. But let me say this: I don't think you guys will have to use this technique. I think Pete will respond better to positive rewards and training tips."

We were feeling anxious once more. We, along with Zippy, relocated to the backyard, where Tim had a big fenced-in space to continue his training demonstration. Durango Pete was happy to be free in the big yard. He ran around like a crazy thing, doing long circular sprints through the grass. Tim called out to Durango Pete, "Durango Pete! Come!"

Of course, Pete ignored Tim's command—and two or three more. He continued his laps around the yard. Tim headed for Pete, walking briskly and continuing to call Pete to come. We followed along behind Tim. After a bit of work, Tim corralled Pete. Pete was shark-eyed and panting.

"Pete, sit!" Tim said firmly. Pete didn't respond. Tim tried again, this time showing a cheese treat. "Pete, sit!" Durango Pete was so wound up, the cheese didn't matter. Tim grasped Pete around his torso and tried to roll him. Pete fought him, desperate to stay upright. Pete's eyes were wild, big, and round, with the whites clearly showing. Tim regripped and tried again. This time he was successful, and Pete was pinned to the grass, belly up but still fighting with all the strength he had.

Tim held Pete there. He began to stroke Pete gently on his flank, and he talked to Pete with a slow, gentle voice, "Easy boy. That's OK, little fella—easy now." He continued to pet Pete and to talk him down with a soothing voice. Pete looked at me. His eyes were still showing his panic. It was horrible to watch.

Then Pete's voice came to me. It was as clear as the day was bright. "Dad, how could you do this to me?"

Finally, Pete let out a big sigh—audible from where Cynthia and I stood. Then he gave in. At least, to an outsider observing the scene, that is how it appeared. I knew better. I think Tim did too. He knew what a force Durango Pete was. Tim picked up on it from the time he first laid eyes on Pete.

"OK, boy. I'm gonna let you up now." Tim released his grip on Pete. Pete wriggled to his feet quickly, and he ran away, gaining some distance. There he stood, ears up, looking at us with his head cocked just enough. I knew what he was thinking.

I did not like the technique. I thought it was ugly and demeaning. I thought to myself, "I will never do this to him."

The first thirty minutes with Tim had flown by. Tim said it was time for Zippy to play with Pete in the backyard. Tim wanted to observe Pete's behavior around another dog—especially another strong-willed cattle dog. Zippy had found shade in the backyard too. He had been sleeping under the deck. Tim called to him, "Zip! Come here, boy!" Zip got up slowly and then trotted over to us. Durango Pete was still keeping some distance between him and us. He watched Zippy approach.

Zippy sized Durango Pete up real fast. Zip was two or three times the size of Pete. Of course, that didn't stop Pete from being his usual annoying, crazy self. The two of them started off with a rousing game of chase. Grass flew. It was a sight to see, our small cattle dog pup chasing and being chased by a full-grown cattle dog. Clearly, they came from the same gene pool. They had the same astounding ability to accelerate from a dead stop to full-speed within ten yards. They each turned on a dime, displaying cutting skills that any NFL halfback would die for. They nipped at heels, as any self-respecting heeler should do.

Soon, though, as it always does with Durango Pete, the benign game of chase turned to darker endeavors. These, of course, were instigated by Pete: wrestling, paw fighting, and sadly—humping.

Zippy was a good sport—until it came to being humped by Durango Pete. It was here that Zip drew the line. Zip barked sharply at Pete, with impressive teeth fully bared. Pete dismounted and immediately dropped to the ground in a submissive pose. Tim was impressed. I was relieved that Pete displayed some discretion and instinctually wise behavior. Zip could have had Pete for lunch.

The hour-long session with Tim soon concluded. All in all, with the exception of the alpha roll, Durango Pete had great fun with Tim and Zippy. Tim reassured us that what we were seeing in Pete was typical cattle dog puppy behavior and that he thought Durango was coming along as should be expected. Tim told us that Pete did display the ability to focus, and that Pete was able to read dog language (from Zippy) and appropriate responses.

Before the session ended, Cynthia and I talked with Tim a little bit about the leash issues we were having with Pete. Tim thought we should start using the leash, or a lead, in the yard for shorter distances and periods of time than a typical walk. He also encouraged us to leave a short leash on Pete in the house so that Pete would get used to the feeling of his collar and leash. We were using a harness versus a collar, and Tim thought we might have better success with a different system, one called an "EasyGO" harness. Finally, Tim recommended that we get a fifty-foot piece of rope and make a slip lead on one end. He said this would come in handy in large, open spaces like Pete's favorite park. It would allow Pete to experience playtime in a fashion similar with that of being off a leash, but the lead would prevent Pete from taking off on us. We would also be able to give him leash input to encourage him to come to us when he was being called from longer distances.

We were encouraged after our session with Tim. We were eager to use the techniques (except the alpha roll) Tim had taught us and to use the suggestions he had made.

Following our training session with Tim, Cynthia and I decided that we would focus on a "one day at a time approach" with Pete. We did this to avoid the depressing thought of living with a crazy dog for another year to two years until he was through the puppy phase and hopefully became calmer. We were going to make a full-blown attempt to live in the moment with Durango Pete. We hoped that, by doing so, we could celebrate and enjoy his successes and not stew about things that might or might not happen in the future.

Soon, following Tim's visit and his suggestion, we purchased an "EasyGO" harness and gave that a try. We were hopeful. We lived in the moment—until we put the new harness on Pete and tried to go for a walk. It was a complete failure. The new harness placed the leash not on his back, but in front of Pete, where it became an easy target for his snapping jaws and teeth. It was a built-in invitation for a big game of tug-of-war, using the leash for play, certainly not for any walking.

We went back to the torso harness for our main walking device. The harness was getting too small, so we bought the next-larger size and continued our daily battle. I was still carrying him for the first two blocks because he refused to leave the house and yard. The distances Pete and I traveled on our walks were increasing gradually, but it was an agonizingly slow process. I still tried a slip-type lead from time to time, never with success. We also began to use a collar in the house and left his short leash on so that Pete might habituate to it.

Many resources we read about cattle dogs talked about how cattle dogs are usually better off a leash than on a leash. It made perfect sense to me. After all, cattle dogs were bred to be on the roam, working the sheep and cattle out in the pasture and fields. I couldn't imagine any dingo being happy about being tethered with a leash. Even though I was concerned about Pete taking off on me, I decided to start giving him short periods of time off his leash on our walks. He was immediately in dog heaven when I did this.

In retrospect, I think this may have been one of the first times that I realized Durango Pete was communicating with me. We were out on our usual route that took us around Crystal Lake, the glorified pond at the center of our suburban neighborhood. It was the kind of October day that we often get in Denver, sunny and cool, with a snap in the air that is bracing and that provides a glimpse of what will come in just a few weeks. I was feeling bright. Pete seemed to be in a similar state of mind.

We walked along the lake path, just the two of us. No one else was out and about. It was midmorning and kids were at school, and parents were at work or busy with chores around the houses. The mountains, a short distance to the west, loomed over us, the way they do when the air is free of dust and other pollution. We made our usual halting progress. I was maintaining a surprising amount of equilibrium. I was enjoying the day and the scenery. Suddenly, an idea leaped into my head: "Let Pete off the leash." Where did that come from? Until that time, I had maintained a death grip on his leash, fearing that, should he come unhooked, he would sprint off and we would never see him again, unless he was squashed by a car as he ran across Rampart Road.

The idea persisted. "Let Pete off leash. You might be surprised." I told Pete to stop. He did. I rewarded him immediately with a cheesy treat and a "good boy, Pete." I kept a good supply of his favorite treats on hand at all times. He was a chow-loving hound, and cheesy treats usually worked to get him focused on me. I reached down and unhooked the leash clasp from the hoop between his shoulder blades. He never looked up at me. He simply trotted up the trail a few yards and exited onto the grass and weeds next to the water to do some fine sniffing. I walked forward to where he was hanging out, with his nose to the ground. "Good boy, Pete," I said. I fished into the treat pouch and gave him another reward and a pat on his head. He took the treat quickly, and then he sauntered a few more yards up the path, until he found something new to sniff and upon which to pee—still using a squatting technique.

We continued forward on the lake path, three yards and a treat, then five yards and a treat. To my surprise, Pete stayed reasonably close to me when he was off his leash. I was shocked—and overjoyed! If Pete got too far behind or ahead, or if he wandered too far to the side, I simply hollered, "Pete—want a treat?" He waited for his cheesy reward. I hooked him back up for the return trip to our house, eager to tell Cynthia about what had happened. Pete waited patiently as I fumbled with the leash clasp. He looked straight ahead, waiting for me to finish. Then a familiar voice jumped into my mind. "Jeesh, Dad. What's the big deal? I told you to unhook me."

It was about this time that Cynthia and I made another great discovery about Durango Pete. In many ways, it is a humorous episode. But despite being funny, the discovery proved very useful.

On another walk, when he was about three months old and after my first off-leash episode, Pete was off his leash again, and he had gotten too far behind me. I hadn't been paying close enough attention to him. I was probably staring off into space and pondering some existential matter. Anyhow, I finally awakened from my reverie and discovered that Pete was highly engaged in his own existential discoveries. I hollered at him, "Pete! Come!" He never looked up from what it was that he was doing. Thinking that he might not have heard my voice, I hollered again, louder even. "Pete! *Come!*" Same thing; no response. I was getting annoyed at his lack of concern about my growing anxiety. I tried again, using treats as a lure. "Durango Pete—come get a treat!"

He had not responded to my "come" commands. He hadn't even responded to my multiple attempts to lure him with treats. Finally, I was fed up with him. I was disgusted and angry that he was ignoring me. I yelled out in frustration and anger, "See ya later!"

I was serious. I was ready to leave him and see what would happen. He must have known I was upset and unhappy with him. Here he came at a full run. He had a look of panic in his eyes. "You were gonna leave me, Dad! What the heck? Please don't leave me, Dad!" Inwardly, I smiled. Pete had divulged a vulnerability. Of course, when he came to me with that panicked look in his eyes, I rubbed him up a bunch, and I told him what a good dog he was and how proud I was of him for coming to me. But I made sure that I put the leash back on him before I made the big scene.

"See ya later!" soon became a regular technique we used to keep Pete close to us during off-leash sessions. It was true that Pete was a little dog with a big attitude. We had learned that early on. But now we were finding out that some of it was false bravado. In some ways, he was a scared little kid, and his panicked return after every "See ya later, Pete!" was perfect evidence of that fact.

The weather, even though it was October, had been mild. So Pete and I spent a fair amount of time each day in our backyard. Because Pete was a herding dog, I decided to buy a big playground ball and see if he would play with it. I thought maybe he would herd it around the backyard. Pete took to this game like a duck to water. He went nuts! He used his nose to push the ball and turn it, and he used his legs and paws to bat the ball or trap it. His ability to accelerate and turn on a dime was unbelievable. His brakes were good too. In fact, he stopped so abruptly that his back end would lift into the air and he would tumble forward into a somersault. We named this new backyard game "cattle ball." When I said, "Pete, get your cattle ball," he knew exactly what do. Pete and I had some great cattle ball games that fall. To this day, it remains one of his favorite things to do. If we forget to put the ball away, and we have gone inside the house to take a rest or do some chores, soon we'll hear Pete's piercing cattle dog yipe— one after another after another. He is playing cattle ball solo style.

Cattle ball was just one of the activities we used so that we could get Pete enough exercise and provide him with some mental stimulation. We continued to work on his tricks, and we tried to add more new activities. Another of Pete's favorite outdoor activities was a game of fetch using a beat-up old flying hoop I had found on one of our walks. This game was good for working on fetch, come, and release. Pete was a very good fetcher. Come and release were not his more accomplished skills. Once again, I had to take advantage of his chowhound weakness and use his favorite treats as motivators and reinforcement. The treats worked very well for the release part of the game but not so well for the come part of the game. He would bring the hoop partway to me, but then the come part devolved into a great game of keep-away. Again, his cattle dog instincts were surfacing. He loved to run, cut, and dodge. Pete came to know this game as "hoop a doop." I could say, "Pete, get your Hoop a Doop!" Off he would go in search of his chewed-up old flying ring.

That fall, I discovered another fact about Durango Pete. Maybe this is true of all puppies. His attention span was annoyingly short. Even his favorite games, like cattle ball and hoop a doop, were only good for about eight repetitions. Then he was off in search of something else of interest, often a unique piece of mulch or working on the hole he was digging to China in the yard. We had to continually change up activities for Pete. It wasn't easy.

Another thing we had read about cattle dogs was the importance of socializing them with other dogs and other people, and to do so in a variety of circumstances. Tim had stressed this too. Motivating Durango Pete to participate in these activities was not difficult. Pete loved people (especially children), loved dogs, and loved to do new things.

If people approached on our walks, Pete immediately refused to go anywhere. He sat there and stayed until he had a chance to say hello.

Our usual walking route, around the Crystal Lake pond, was popular with other residents. During the day, Pete and I mostly encountered other retired folks. Sometimes they were walking their own dogs. One of the first fellow residents, and fellow graybeard, whom Pete and I met was Dale. I can always spot Dale from a distance because he walks like me—stiff from too many years and too many hard jobs and fun. Anyway, Dale has a dog of his own. She is a small terrier the color of ginger. Appropriately, that is her name. Ginger runs the show at Dale's house. And she considers the Crystal Lake trail an extension of her house. She doesn't walk on a leash. No self-respecting dog or neighborhood chief would. Every day, she inspects the pond. She does a fine job.

On that particular day, Pete spotted Dale and Ginger walking on the opposite side of the lake. They were headed in the opposite direction from us. We would soon cross paths. Durango Pete seemed to know this. But he stopped periodically to size up the situation, making certain that they were still headed toward us. Shortly, Dale and Ginger were within easy shouting distance. Pete stopped. He walked his front paws forward, until he was crouching on his belly, front legs extended forward and his hind legs tucked under, appearing ready to spring. I waited with Pete as they got closer and closer. I shortened the lead, not knowing exactly what to expect from Pete.

Ginger walked up first. She was a bit wary, I could see. But she was anything but shy. Pete's butt rose up slightly.

When Ginger was within striking distance, Pete leaped forward! Ginger stopped dead in her tracks. Despite his stalking antics and his crazy leap, Pete simply circled around Ginger, his tail and rump wiggling happily from side to side. For her part, Ginger circled too—in place—to make sure she had him continuously in sight. Dale came up next. He said, "Hello!" Pete forgot all about Ginger. Before I could reply, and before I could reel Pete back in, he jumped up on Dale using his front paws, and he struck Dale a direct blow to his private parts.

I was horrified. I reeled Pete in, and I apologized profusely. Dale was a good sport. He said it was no big deal, and he got down on one knee (way better than I could) and gave Pete plenty of rubs and scratches on Pete's scruff.

Introductions were properly made. More apologies were given by me. Pete was pretty much oblivious to it all. Ginger, for her part, was stoic and polite. She clearly was not to be messed with, though, and Pete appeared to get the message, for he never tried to hump her or rough her up. We managed to part ways with no serious damage done. To this day, despite our friendship with Ginger and Dale, and our familiarity, Pete tries to rack Dale every time.

After our first Dale and Ginger encounter, meetings with other humans walking their dogs became routine chances for us to work on the "off" command—although not with much success.

During this first fall with Durango Pete, Cynthia and I discovered that there were two times each day that Pete loved to be outside and on his own in the backyard. The first was in the morning when the kids were walking to school. The second was their return at the close of the school day. Pete sat in the mulched garden by the back fence, and he watched the parade come and go. In the early days, Pete didn't engage in too much barking and running up and down the fence line. That behavior came later, after he had spent some time with Cyrus in our yard. Cyrus would teach Pete the joys of fence sprints, especially when the UPS or FedEx trucks sped by on the street behind our house. But before that, in the early days, we came to find out that he was building quite a fan club among the people who passed by.

Children are typically attracted to dogs. Durango Pete was no exception. He was clearly a puppy, and that made him less intimidating. Plus, he is pleasing to the eye and has a certain way about him that garners attention. Somehow, several of the kids had discovered his name. Stopping by our fence on the way home became a daily ritual for them. I suspect a treat or two might have endeared them to Pete. What the treats were that the kids gave him, I can only imagine.

Another routine visitor to the fence was a dog named Pepper and her owner, Sharon. One day, Pete and I were lounging in the family room, enjoying the fall sun that was streaming in through the big glass sliding door that overlooked our backyard. Suddenly, Pete was up and at the door, whining incessantly. I arose to see what the fuss was all about. An elegant-looking woman with beautiful silver hair was walking her small, black dog past our back fence. The little black terrier led the way. The elegant woman followed behind resolutely at the far end of her ten-foot leash. Pete was beside himself. I let him out before he could do permanent damage to the sliding door. He sprinted down the deck stairs and across the lawn to greet the little dog and woman. I cracked the door slightly and observed.

Truth be known, Pete gave the small black terrier short shrift. Pete sprinted up to the woman. He promptly sat on his haunches in the mulch, ears up, and he looked at her and waited. It appeared to me that Pete knew her. Then I heard her exclaim, "Oh, Durango! There you are! Good morning. I see that you want a treat." Pete didn't reply. He knew what was coming. She reached into her pocket for something. As the prize emerged, I could see that it was some sort of bacon-looking dog treat. It was substantial. When he saw it, Pete jumped onto the fence with his front paws. He was too small still to reach the top. The lady tossed the treat over the fence. Pete grabbed it midair, and the treat disappeared in one mighty gulp. He sat once again and looked at her. "Oh, Durango!" I heard her say. "My, my you are a hungry boy. OK, one more treat, and that's all." Once again, she tossed the large bacon treat over the fence. Once again, Pete snatched it out of the air, and it was immediately gone. As before, Pete sat down at in the mulch at the base of the fence. Hope springs eternal. But alas, two treats were all that there was to be given. "Bye-bye, Pete!" she said in a big, happy voice. Down the sidewalk she went, silver hair shining in the sunlight and her little black dog leading the way. Pete remained in his spot until the woman and her dog were long out of sight. Then he walked slowly back to the sliding door, where I stood watching.

As winter approached, the number of good days Cynthia and I had with Pete was increasing. However, Pete was still a moving target and full of surprises. Within each day, we had good times, and we had bad times. The evenings were usually the worst. Every evening at about 7 p.m., Durango Pete went into his shark-eye phase. When his eyes went black, we braced ourselves for the inevitable. Pete ran through the house like a crazy dog. Back and forth and around and around he went—full speed. It was amazing to watch. I have since discovered that there is a name for this behavior. It is called "orbiting." Not only did Pete orbit, but he also barked a lot. Along with the barking and orbiting, Pete nipped and bit at our hands, feet, heels, shoes, socks, pant legs, and anything else within reach of his snapping shark mouth. When Pete did this, there was no restraining him physically. Food and treats had no effect. The only thing that worked was to put him in his kennel that we had named the shark cage. Every evening was a repeat of the evening before. Each evening, we could see the behavior escalate. Soon, there was the inevitable explosion followed by our failed attempts to restore calm and order to the household, and finally we had to relegate our little cattle dog-turned-shark to his shark cage for a time-out.

We were in the habit of moving Pete's kennel to our bedroom in the evening at bedtime—and then back to the family room every morning after we were up for the day. Maybe Pete had a vendetta against his kennel because of his frequent banishment to it, or perhaps it was his ancient cattle dog genes manifesting themselves. Every time we moved the kennel (shark cage), Pete started herding the kennel—biting at the cage and growling and yapping at it as we went.

One night, after Pete's usual volcanic eruption of craziness and zooming, and after we had retrieved his cage and brought it into the family room for his nightly time-out, Pete attacked the cage once again. For some reason, on that evening the song from *Rawhide* came into my head. It was the theme song from a good old western television show, complete with horses and cows. I began to sing as Cynthia and I tried to move the cage, with Pete growling and biting the metal cross-hatching.

> *"Rollin', rollin', rollin',*
> *With his cage we're strollin',*
> *Keep this doggie rollin',*
> *Sharkhide!"*

Pete, being a cattle dog, seemed to enjoy this. Now our nightly "shark cage roundup" had a theme song. Every night, Pete went shark-eye. Every night, Cynthia and I headed to the bedroom to retrieve the shark cage. Every night, Pete tried to herd the hated steel prison. Every night, I broke into song.

The first signs of winter were upon us. The leaves were largely gone from the trees, and the grasses on the mountains close to the west had gone golden. With the onset of November, Durango Pete celebrated the start of his fourth month since his birth in New Mexico. He had been with us for two months and a week.

I was starting to feel like I was making some progress in establishing myself as the head honcho of our little goat rodeo. He was doing less mouthing and biting of me, especially during times of play on the floor. He was starting to respond to my commands to "stop" when he was engaged in inappropriate behaviors. Cynthia was not having the same success. In fact, it seemed like his behaviors were escalating with her. It was now impossible for her to sit down in the family room or lie down on the family room couch without Pete harassing her. It was as if Pete saw Cynthia as his personal chew toy. She started to get serious about correcting this obnoxious behavior. She used the "ouch" response; then she ignored him. If he persisted, he was on the three-strikes-and-you-are-out program. The third time he was corrected, he went immediately to the shark cage—in the other room. After a bit of solitary confinement, Pete was released, and we would start all over again. Sometimes this was effective and sometimes it was not.

We still did not feel a strong bond forming between Pete and us. Pumpkin had followed us everywhere. She only needed to be with us. Other than food, our company was all that mattered to her. We knew that she loved us. Such signs of attachment were rare with Durango Pete. It was unsettling to think that we had spent so much time, effort, and money on Pete, yet we still, after several months, didn't know if we meant more to him than a meal ticket and shelter. We shared feeding responsibilities, and we traded off on walking Pete—or tried to take him walking with both of us. We both worked on his tricks. We wanted Pete to develop an attachment to both of us. In spite of this, it seemed like he could take us or leave us. Our feeling that he didn't need us—or even like us—was a stab in our hearts. After all, everything we read talked about how attached to their owners cattle dogs become. This is not what we saw. I lay in bed at night, Pete in his kennel or on the floor, thinking about him. I was starting to wonder who or what was inside of this wild, little cattle dog. What made him tick? What were his first six weeks in New Mexico like? Was he essentially a feral dog? At last I thought,

"Did he give a damn about us?" Many nights I fell asleep with these thoughts swirling about in my head.

I thought about Tim the Trainer. I remembered how he had commented on Durango's eyes the day he was working with Pete. When the sun hit Durango's eyes just right, they turned a crazy, piercing yellow. It was unsettling and eerie. Tim had stated that maybe there was some wolf in Durango Pete. I started to wonder the same thing. Maybe that would explain his reluctance to bond with us, his struggle to dominate Cynthia and me, and the periodic explosions of crazy behavior. Sometimes Pete would look at me in a way that was so wild and ancient—and so wise and frightening. I began to call him *el perro del Diablo*, the dog of the Devil.

One afternoon in November, Durango and I were outside lounging around in the backyard, basking in the sun. After a while, I arose, and I went on poop patrol, which had become a daily chore. Pete's digestive system was outsized, like his personality. After I had completed cleaning up his messes, we played some fetch with his tennis ball. When he became bored with that, we played some hoop a doop, and we played a rousing game of cattle ball. The cattle ball really got Pete wound up. He started biting at my feet, ankles, and pants legs. None of my usual commands worked to stop him. As I got more and more frustrated and failed to stop his biting, he got crazier and crazier. Finally, he bit my ankle so hard that it hurt. Before I knew it, I had him on the ground, and I tried to alpha roll him. Pete fought like crazy. The look in his eyes was absolutely feral and wild. Even so, I got him to his back and then his side. I was so angry! I was tired of him challenging us and attacking us out of the blue. I held him firm, pinned to the ground so he could not escape. His eyes rolled back, his nostrils flared wide, and his breathing was ragged. I could feel his heart going a hundred miles an hour. He struggled some more. Then, after what seemed like minutes, he finally gave up. I talked to him and tried to calm him down. After a while, I released some of my pressure, and he did not fight. I let him up slowly.

He was no longer crazy. But despite his calmer behavior, I felt terrible. I felt something had broken between us. Instead of feeling closer to Pete, I felt I had forced him even further away. I was not confident that doing the alpha roll had been smart. I felt bad that I had done it.

I would like to say that this was the only time I used the alpha roll with Durango Pete. It was not. We had entered a very difficult period.

Pete became a wild man around strangers and dogs who approached him. He wasn't mean; he was much more out of control in public. Behaviors that had been largely confined to our house, and with us, became manifested in public places. When he met people on the path or in the park, he jumped on them and ran around them and between their legs. He could not restrain himself, and restraining him was difficult. I was afraid to give him much length on his leash. I kept him close to me, and I was constantly looking over my shoulder and ahead for people approaching.

Beyond that, he was still attacking Cynthia at night and going after my ankles and feet during our backyard sessions and during our on-leash walks. Every time we crossed an intersection on our leash walks, he attacked my ankles and pants legs. Additionally, leash walking was now a never-ending game of tug-of-war. One leash was already nearly bitten through. Once again, I started to dread walking with Pete. Cynthia dreaded the evenings and Durango Pete's attacks on her and his shark-eye zooming and craziness.

My patience was wearing thin. My nerves were shot, and I was anxious around Pete much of the time, waiting for the next explosion of behaviors and challenges to my authority and control. At least two more times at home, my anger erupted, and I rolled Pete as Tim had demonstrated. Each time I got frustrated to the point of rolling him, Pete got more stubborn than before. It became harder and harder to get him to give in. He remained agitated and combative longer and longer. I couldn't get him to relax, no matter how much I tried to talk him down or how much I tried to soothe him by stroking his flank. Pinning him to the ground was demoralizing and heartbreaking.

I never rolled Pete in public. Instinctively, I knew that the technique was borderline abusive. My anger at his escalating behaviors was not so easy to contain at home, and the alpha roll was far more accessible without the scrutiny and judgment of people on the street and in the park. Each time I used it inside our home, or in our backyard, I was crushed inside. In addition to my own anguish in using the technique, the alpha roll also seemed to be causing even crazier behavior in Pete. He hated it. I hated it. I feared that Pete was beginning to fear me—possibly even hate me. I was depressed. Pete and I had entered a great struggle.

CHAPTER 5

TIM THE TRAINER RETURNS

ONE DAY I WAS DOING some research online about cattle dogs, dog behavior, and training techniques. I stumbled across a story by a fellow who had been trying to use the alpha roll with his dog. He was having the same sort of escalating difficulties that I was having with Durango Pete. The man felt that the use of the roll was creating a divide between him and his dog. He had made a gut-level decision to stop. In fact, he decided to get down on the floor with his dog and let his dog win during a floor-play activity. He let his dog get on top of him! I had always been warned by other trainers familiar with cattle dogs to never let them win in any game or battle of wills. Many experts on the breed were clear about the dangers of playing on the floor with them—at their level. The suggestions recommended playing the games from a standing or seated position to maintain a dominant position in space. I had only played tug-of-war with Pete from a standing or seated position. I had never played the game on the floor. I had never allowed Pete to win either. I had always ended up pulling the rope from him, or I had persisted until he gave in.

I could not believe that I had found this story. The man's experiences with his cattle dog were just like mine with Durango Pete. It was serendipity! After reading, and after my own experiences with the rolling technique, I knew that I was never going to alpha roll Pete again. I hated how it made me feel, and I hated the look I saw in Durango Pete's eyes each time I did it.

The very afternoon after I had read the story, I got down on the floor and started playing tug-of-war with Pete. He was startled to see me there, on the floor with him. I grabbed his favorite rope, and we rollicked on the carpet. It was the first time I had played tug on his level, and it was the first time I had let Pete crawl all over the top of me. Then, as we battled there on the floor, I let him pull the rope out of my grasp. It was the first time I had ever let him win.

I cannot describe the look on Pete's face that afternoon during our play on the floor. We had a great time rolling on the carpet. I found out that Pete was not a crazy tug-of-war player. In fact, he played a lazy game of tug. He either wore out quickly, or he was fully satisfied after a few minutes of rough play. After the full-blown tug-of-war battle, Pete preferred to lie down on his side and have me dangle the rope in front of him. There, he could grab it with his paws and chew on any loose strands for a few minutes. Then he wanted me to dangle it again. After ten minutes or so, he was satisfied.

From then on, we played "lazy tug" every day. I swear, that day on the floor was a turning point in our relationship. It was then that a bond started to develop between Durango Pete and me. Much later, when Pete and I were out and about on this adventure or that adventure, this theme would visit us again and again, the eternal struggle for control and dominance. As for Pete and me, that struggle would continue despite our breakthrough on the floor.

Whether this was a sign that our relationship with Durango Pete was advancing, or was simply my love for words and word play, Durango Pete began to accumulate lots of nicknames. I confess that I have always loved nicknames. Almost all my friends, from childhood through high school, had nicknames. The "Sloth," "Ace," and "Dude" (I also call my wife "Dude") were friends of mine. "The Root," "Poiyea," "The Weasel," "Clammy," and "Bombo" were also part of the gang in high school. Even my dad had a nickname—given to him by his loving sons. Dad's nickname was "The Ogre," or simply "The Oge" in the interest of brevity.

Our previous dog, Pumpkin, had generated an unbelievable number of nicknames over eighteen years. Some of our favorites were "Lips Manlich," "Esmerelda Pranceworthy the Third," "Twinkle Toes Jones," "Mrs. Ohlmert," and of course, "Punky Lou."

It was only natural that Durango Pete (although his name is certainly awesome enough) would start to accumulate a few nicknames of his own. One of the earliest was given to him by our two-year-old granddaughter. She called Pete "Mango Mango." Other early nicknames for Durango Pete included "Dingobat," "Wild Bill Hiccups"

(Pete had chronic hiccups), "Munchkin Toast," and "Petey Pie." Of course, there was "El Diablo," appropriate for the times when his ears stood straight up like horns and when his eyes glowed yellow. He looked the perfect part of a devil—not to mention his possessed behavior.

In early November, I started to worry about how Pete would fare once the weather started to get very cold and the snow started to fly. I was concerned that we would not be able to get Pete enough exercise to satisfy his needs and keep him from becoming bored and getting into trouble. It was a sobering thought.

Durango Pete was growing like a weed. He had about doubled in size since we got him. His ears had been floppy when we first adopted him. They were so cute when they were still folded over. But soon after his arrival, one ear had popped up. It was a huge ear. Not long after the first ear popped up, the second ear popped up too. My goodness! His ears were giant. He looked like a jackrabbit. I now had a dog with the very kind of ears I had complained about. It must have been fate playing a big, funny trick on me. I hoped that someday he would grow into his rabbit ears because he looked like a cartoon character. Pete was all ears, like the greeting card characters Hoops and Yoyo.

Cynthia and I had been making slow but steady progress with Pete's walking—on a leash and off a leash. He was far from perfect, but at least we could go on walks, provided we had a fully stocked treat pouch with us that was packed to the brim with his favorite treats. But one should never get too content or smug when training a cattle dog.

Pete now seemed to have no interest in leaving the house to walk, or even walking on a leash when we drove him to interesting outdoor areas. We gathered his walking gear up, treat bag and all, and we went to the front door. Pete sat in the family room looking at us. We called to him, "Pete! Let's go for a walk!" There he remained. We encouraged him with treats. There he remained. We were happy that Pete liked his house, but he needed to walk. What dog doesn't like to go for walks?

Cynthia and I loved to exercise outside. We hiked, we ran, we backpacked, we snowshoed and cross-country skied, and we cycled. Pumpkin had joined us on most of these adventures. She had done hikes and runs that were eight to ten miles in length. She had climbed several peaks with us. We had expected that Durango Pete would also join us on our adventures and that he would enjoy them. After all, he was a cattle dog! But we still had big problems. It seemed impossible that we could do the things we had done with Pumpkin if Pete's leash-walking problems could not be solved.

After weeks of struggling to get Durango Pete to leave the house and walk on a leash, we finally decided to give Tim, our cattle dog trainer, a call. We thought Tim might be able to help us with Pete's leash walking. Tim said he would be happy to work with us and Pete again, and he would bring Zippy along to help with the training.

On the appointed day and time, Tim rolled up to the front of our house in his rusty but trusty pickup truck. Cynthia and I could see that he was wearing the same baseball cap as before, and we could see Zippy's cattle dog ears sticking up in the truck cab. We greeted Tim and Zip like long-lost friends.

Tim told us that he thought Durango Pete might be reluctant to leave the house because it was Pete's "den." Tim believed if we made walking attractive enough, we might be able to overcome his reluctance. Tim wanted to start the session using the EasyGO harness we had purchased. So, we put it on Pete, and Tim attached the leash. No go. Pete put on his brakes, and that was the end of the EasyGO. Tim decided that we should put a regular collar on Pete and try that. Durango Pete now had his regular collar on, and we had his retractable leash and his regular leash to try. This went a little better than the EasyGO, but Pete's performance was still not what we expected and certainly not what Tim expected from a cattle dog. Usually, cattle dogs are doing the pulling on the leash instead of the owner dragging the dog along to get from point A to point B. Tim suggested that one of us man the leash and the other person walk in front of Pete with a treat, to lure him forward. Since Cynthia was having a harder time than I was having with Pete on a leash, Tim wanted her to be the walker, and I would be the target with the treat.

What torture this was! Pete was sort of motivated to move forward, but not much. We made progress in very small increments—three feet and a treat, two feet and another treat, and then a sit-down strike. We repeated this again and again, with me bent over waving a treat in front of Pete's nose. My back was killing me. Tim could not believe it. He had never encountered a cattle dog reluctant to walk, let alone one reluctant to walk when a treat was involved.

After twenty minutes or so of this frustrating exercise, with both of us taking turns at the helm, Tim stopped the activity. He mulled things over for a minute or two. He brightened. Tim decided to try using Zippy to motivate Pete. Tim rigged up a way to tether Durango Pete to Zippy, hoping that Pete would then follow Zippy along. Zip had no problem walking on a leash. Off Zippy went. Not so much Durango Pete. Pete had the brakes on so hard that he was being dragged down the street by Zippy, in a full-on four-wheel skid. I was surprised there wasn't smoke coming from Pete's paws. Tim tried rigging the two dogs together in a variety of ways. None of them worked. Zippy was certainly getting tired of dragging this obstinate little cattle dog around. So far the score in leash walking was Pete—2, Tim the Trainer and us—0.

I think Tim was getting a bit frustrated. I didn't blame him. We certainly were frustrated. Tim removed his brown ball cap with the well-curled and soiled brim. His red hair was happy to escape the confines of the cap. It sprung out this way and that, relieved to be so free. Tim slowly reached up and scratched his head, thinking about this dilemma. Finally, he said, "Here's what we're gonna do, guys. We're gonna throw the treats out in front of Durango Pete to get that ornery little cuss moving forward. And that ain't all, guys! We need a lot of treats, cuz we're gonna keep tossin' 'em as long as need be—to keep Pete movin'!"

We grabbed Pete's treat bag, took it inside, and filled it to the brim with the best treats—mostly cheese. Zip lay down in some shade and watched the circus unfold.

Off we went, three adults and Pete, down the street, us throwing treats in front of Durango as we went, all the time hollering, "Get the treat, Pete! Get the treat, Pete!" Pete seemed to respond to this technique. We made progress of sorts. However, our line of progression reflected the roll and direction that each treat would take after our toss. So we hardly moved in anything resembling a straight line. Of course, if we didn't keep throwing the treats soon enough, or often enough, Pete would simply sit down and refuse to move until we freed another morsel from the treat pouch. "What sort of behavior were we reinforcing?" I thought. "Were we encouraging walking or sitting?"

Somehow, we managed to reserve enough treats that we successfully circled back and arrived home without tapping out. Zippy watched the whole show from his prone position in the grass. The hour had gone by quickly. We weren't sure about the new walking strategy that Tim had developed. We were sure, however, that the technique had been a last-ditch, desperate move on his part. We were entirely sympathetic. It must have been quite a sight for the neighbors. After this, our walking sessions became known as "going treat tossing."

We thanked Tim for his help. He wished us good luck, saying in parting, "Yes, sir, that Pete is one of a kind. Oh, he's a cattle dog all right, but I think he's a bit more too." Tim hauled himself up into the pickup cab, Zip next to him on the bench seat. He adjusted his ball cap so that the red hair sprouted from underneath here and there. Then he fired up the engine and lumbered away, and for the time being we were once again on our own. Cynthia, Pete, and I continued our schedule. Durango Pete got us up at 6:30 a.m. for our morning potty break and breakfast. It wasn't a polite awakening. He jumped on our necks, gave us a paw swipe or two, and then licked our faces hard enough to peel skin back. After bathroom and breakfast, Pete took a nap in his doggy bed in front of the fireplace while I did some writing. When he started to get restless, I saved my work, put away the computer, and went to the kitchen to get his collar and leash.

Cynthia and I had been diligent about using the treat-tossing technique with Durango Pete. Restocking treats from Petco was getting expensive, but Pete's walking became somewhat better in the late fall. Unfortunately, he still had the bad habit of biting the leash as soon as we turned around to head back home or to the car. Now that he was walking more and appearing to like it even though we had begun to taper the frequency of treat tossing, was he now upset and acting out when he knew we were headed home and the walk would be ending? He was so exasperating!

This leash-biting habit had gotten to the point that I was desperate for some solution. Twice we had nearly been hit by approaching cars when we were in crosswalks and Pete had abruptly stopped and had begun biting the leash, growling, and pulling on it.

I researched this behavior on the Internet, and I found a variety of recommendations. I had already considered switching from the rope-style slip lead to a metal chain-style leash. I had tried the retractable leash, and it was no better than the rope leash. I figured that Durango would not enjoy biting the leash if he got a mouth full of metal. Many of the recommendations I read suggested using a chain leash. Off I went to the pet store to purchase a new metal leash, even more treats, and whatever else caught my eye, of course. I had already discovered that the pet store was much the same for me as a hardware store—I liked to browse, looking for solutions to Pete's many behaviors.

In addition to the leash biting, Pete was still periodically biting at our pants legs, cuffs, and shoes. Like biting the leash, this usually took place in the later stages of the walks, when we were starting home or back to the car. These two behaviors were taking most of the fun out of our twice-per-day outings. Whether we were walking or playing at home, we tried to disrupt these behaviors by turning our backs to him and stopping the activity. Or we tried to change his focus by having him do some of his tricks. Neither of these interventions was very successful. And on top of this, he started barking at us at the same time, using his most annoying cattle dog ear-piercing yap. We had been successful in reducing the number of treats we had to toss, but then there were these behaviors. He still baffled me.

Late November arrived. Durango Pete had been in our family for eight or nine weeks. He was such a mystery. Did he love us? Did he want to be with us beyond the fact that we were his source of food? There was no doubt that he was very, very food focused and motivated. He reminded me of a bully in some ways. He put on a good front, displaying a big attitude and lots of bravado. But I was getting a feeling that it was false swagger and bravado. I decided that I would try to connect with him through telepathy or visual images. I still wondered what circumstances he had experienced in New Mexico. Perhaps an answer about what made Durango Pete tick was to be found in his ancestry, his birth circumstances, and his first five to six weeks spent in New Mexico.

We knew nothing about his background before he was relocated to Colorado. I started getting pictures in my head about Pete's environment and the circumstances that had greeted his birth. I got the feeling that he was not brought into the world in loving circumstances. I thought there might be a way to find out more about Pete's entrance to the world.

Years back, I had read the book *Kinship with All Life* by J. Allen Boone. It is the story of Boone, a Hollywood screenwriter, who agreed to take care of a famous movie dog named Strongheart. The author was not experienced with dogs prior to taking on the assignment. Through Strongheart, Boone came to believe that there is a kinship with all living beings and that it is possible to communicate with animals and they with us. He came to the realization that he could communicate with Strongheart through mental images. He learned that by being open and displaying humility, love, and kindness, he developed a unique bond with Strongheart. *Kinship* is a wonderful story and one worth reading, especially for those who love dogs and other animals.

During quiet moments, when I was sitting next to Durango Pete looking at him, I had gotten images of his living circumstances in New Mexico. These images were of red dirt, broken down shelters, and little dog-human interaction. Again, I wondered if he was possibly a reservation dog. I did a bit of research and came to learn that there may be as many as 445,000 feral dogs on the Navajo reservation.

I was keeping a daily diary of my interactions with Durango Pete and the training and walks that Pete and I were doing. In the diary, I had put together a list of the images or intuitions I had been getting about Durango's background and his personality. Here is the list I gathered over time.

- ✍ Reservation dog? Perhaps not feral but neglected?
- ✍ Stressful introduction to the world! No love or trust.
- ✍ His parents had similar experiences in the world and with humans?
- ✍ He was anxious and fearful (yelling would be counterproductive).
- ✍ So *smart*—and a mind reader!
- ✍ He is a changeling? He morphs from moment to moment and day to day.
- ✍ He is an athlete with amazing speed, agility, and balance. Needs to use and challenge those skills.
- ✍ Was Durango Pete a messenger? Was he part of why I had felt so compelled to move back home to Colorado from Kansas City? Were we meant to go through this struggle together?

As I put the list together, I often wondered what the future held for us and Durango Pete.

Durango was around eight weeks old at the time we adopted him. Assuming it took a week to arrange the transfer from New Mexico to Colorado, and if he had spent a week with a foster family, Durango would have been about six weeks old at the time he was separated from his mother. That was terribly young. He did have his siblings with him at the adoption event where we found him. I was concerned that some of Durango's behaviors might be related to his early separation from his mother. But I also believed that some of what I was seeing in Durango might be genetic, especially if his parents were semiferal or semiwild. Some of the behaviors that concerned me and Cynthia were excessive biting during play, eating animal feces and nonfood items, excessive startle reflexes and reactivity to noises, general overstimulation and overregistration of sensory input, excessive sensory-seeking behaviors, reluctance to accept affection and petting, wolfing down his food, excessive jumping on people and dogs, reluctance to walk on a leash, explosive behaviors, and bouts of energy. These behaviors had been present from the first day we had brought Pete home. Now, on top of these, we had the leash biting and ankle biting while walking to add to the list.

My wife and I began to discuss contacting an "animal whisperer" who we knew in Kiowa, Colorado. We had used her before when we wanted to get a better handle on our dog at the time, Pumpkin, and our cat, Rocky. Of course, many of our friends and family thought we were a bit kooky using an animal communicator. But we had been amazed by the things that she had known about Pumpkin and Rocky, considering that she had never met them and that she had been given very little information about them either. We were especially thankful for the insight she had provided us when Pumpkin and Rocky were approaching the end of their lives, when we were struggling with the difficult choices and decisions that we all face when our much-loved pets are at the end of their earthly journeys.

I hemmed and hawed and put off the phone call for several days. I introduced the new leash to Durango Pete, and it did help. He almost never bit the leash once he had been introduced to it. He didn't care for a mouthful of metal links. Instead of biting the leash, he increased the biting of our pants, ankles, and shoes; and he was barking at us even more. I was starting to feel overwhelmed by Durango

Pete once again. Finally, nearing the end of my rope, I decided to call the animal communicator. I left a message for her. I did not divulge more than the fact that we had a new dog and that we were trying to learn more about his background.

Soon she returned my call. She had been given his name. She knew that we had adopted him and that he was from New Mexico originally. Immediately, she said that she was getting an image about him. She said that it was circular in nature and the image was of an explosion. She said, "Oh, my! He has an attitude, and he is a bully." She went on to tell me that he was narcissistic, very street savvy, and extremely smart. So far, this all was consistent with what we were seeing in Durango Pete. She said that Durango was in tune with nature but that he had a hard time focusing on any single thing. She thought that he might have a disorder of some sort related to his mother's lack of good nutrition and poor feeding of him. This is the point at which she told me about the images she was getting about his New Mexico circumstances. She told me that Durango's mom was very short-tempered—a step from being a feral dog. His mother was not treated well and was undernourished. Her meals typically consisted of a bone with very little meat on it—tossed into her pen now and then. As a result, his mom was not able to provide much milk to her litter. She had little energy or interest in yet another litter of puppies. The animal communicator told me that the mom, Durango, and his siblings were kept in a small pen with dirt floors in a very rough neighborhood.

I was amazed at how similar her descriptions of Durango Pete, and his circumstances in New Mexico, were to the images and intuition I was getting about his past and his personality. She told me that Durango Pete was going to be a handful. She said that he would need a lot of variety in his life and that he would need to be challenged intellectually and physically. She talked to me about contacting Ted Kerasote, the author of *Merle's Door*. Merle was wild in nature—similar to Durango Pete. She also gave me two other resources for assistance with training Durango. One of the resources was a woman who had a ranch on the outskirts of Denver. This lady was in the business of training border collies to compete in herding trials and competitions.

Finally, she told me that Durango was in my life to teach me how to use my natural skills, and I was in his life to teach him how to live in the civilized world. She added that Durango felt walking with a leash was "so bourgeois." I thanked her for her time and her help. Then, to my amazement, she concluded by telling me that I should write a book about my adventures with Durango Pete. She told me not to wait until he had passed away to tell the story. She said, "Start now—and make it a series of books."

How did she know? I had already started writing this story. I had said nothing to her about it. She had been accurate in her description of Durango Pete's personality and behaviors. She had described circumstances in New Mexico that were similar to the images I had been getting about Pete's birth and his parents. I had never considered that she might have predictive, psychic skills with humans—similar to those she exhibited with animals. I had been sitting in my easy chair near our fireplace as I talked with her. This particular chair was where I did much of my writing about Durango Pete. In fact, the notebook that contained my notes about Pete, my journal, and my cattle dog research sat opened and on the shelf next to me as I had talked with her. Her comments about writing a book about my experiences with Durango Pete were reinforcing, and they made me wonder once again: was there some sort of destiny at work behind the entry of Durango Pete into my life, and mine into his?

CHAPTER 6

A MUTTUAL UNDERSTANDING

W E COME INTO THE WORLD largely who we are. My brothers and I came from the same seeds, but we are not much the same, and it was that way even when we were young kids. Were my father and mother alive, I am certain that they would agree and that they would say it had been that way from the very beginning. I am blessed with three kids of my own and five grandchildren. They are each unique in who they are, and as it was with my brothers and me, so it is with my own children and grandchildren.

Why, then, would it be different with dogs? I have had three dogs as an adult man. Each of them has been unique and different, not only in breed, but in personality: likes, dislikes, fears, and in their relationships and their bonds with me. I needed to remember that. I needed to allow Durango Pete to be who he was (within some practical boundaries).

One morning, not long after my conversation with the animal communicator, I made my usual large cup of coffee to start the day, and I sat down in my easy chair by the fireplace. Pete was still sleeping. Lately, he had developed the welcome habit of sleeping in. I looked outside and saw that the leaves were fully off the trees and that the grass had taken on the golden tint that heralds winter. "Where had the past few months gone?" I wondered. Of course, I knew the answer: Durango Pete. I nursed the hot coffee, and I thought more about Durango Pete, about myself, and about our relationship.

There were many issues that were illuminated that morning on my journey inward. It came to me like a lightning bolt that my focus, in truth, had been mostly on me since we had brought Durango Pete home. Oh sure, I thought. The things that I had been doing in training Pete were all about him—about him being successful and fitting into life with humans in a simple, suburban home. I had thought that if I shaped him into what my image was of a *good dog*, I would be the hero who saved him from being returned to an agency. And who knew what might be done to him if that were to happen. I had created a dishonest inner dialogue. I had, as a friend once stated, created my own convenient fiction. Pete was the flawed soul who was admirably rescued by me. He was my project, a rough and tumble little bully that I was to make successful. It was a Pavlovian nightmare.

I sank lower into the big chair as the truth hit me right between my eyes. All of this, so far, had largely been about me. I was the hero who had plucked Pete from any of a variety of imaginable but undesirable fates. I was the woebegone old fellow who had made—and was making—huge sacrifices on behalf of a dog who appeared to be thankless and aloof. Oh, how I had suffered! Oh, how I suffered yet!

I took a long sip of the strong coffee. My reflection continued.

Was it a relationship? After all, in any true relationship that is functional and wholesome, there is a give and take, there is compromise, and—most important of all—both partners' needs are considered and met. One cannot simply be the master, and the other the beast. That is slavery. And slavery will always crumble.

What was it that I had truly given Durango Pete? When did I fully explore who he was and what he needed? When had I put myself in his four paws? Finally, what was I willing to give up—what generous sacrifices was I willing to make so that Pete could express that which was in his soul and experience that which he needed? I knew the answers. It started with relinquishing control. I had to open my mind and my heart. I must see Durango Pete as a thinking, feeling, intelligent being, and I must ask him, "Durango Pete, what is it that you need? How can I help you?"

I can tell you now that the day by the fireplace as Durango Pete slept was the beginning of the real story of a man and his dog companion. The joyful part of my adventures with Durango Pete began on that late fall day. The gift and the work of my introspection as I sat by the fire gave birth to the seed out of which would grow my love and respect for Durango Pete. The realization that Durango Pete deserved no less than that which I felt I deserved allowed me to receive the gift and the joy that he is. And the blossoming of a spiritual partnership and journey began. I think it was the same for Durango Pete. Ask him. He will tell you.

I am not going to say that all our battles, Durango Pete's and mine, magically disappeared that day. That would be another convenient fiction. We still had our moments. But a heaviness had been lifted from me. And it appeared that a certain lightness of heart and being grew in Pete as well. For me, the small stuff became small stuff. The big stuff became "How can I allow Durango Pete to express his nature in a safe and appropriate way?" I knew that he had a wild streak that was being smothered. Walks in the neighborhood were nice for exercise, but I knew that he needed a chance to run and be in places that were more natural. Pete was bored. I was bored with the same old familiar paths and routines. We both needed some wild time.

Pete and I started small. But it was a good start. Cynthia and I live only three-quarters of a mile from a geologic uplift that becomes the Dakota Hogback and the foothills that herald the beginning of the Rocky Mountains in Colorado. The weather had turned cold as December replaced November. Our first Thanksgiving with Pete passed. Christmas was around the corner. With the onset of colder weather, the prairie rattlesnakes, which were abundant on the Hogback (the formation's ridge looks like the back of a hog, although in places there are multiple parallel ridges, separated by narrow valleys), had gone to their dens underground. People were less inclined to be out hiking in the brisk weather too. It was a fine time for Durango Pete and me to do some exploring of the wild spaces close to home.

One morning, as the day dawned gray and as the first flakes of snow drifted down from skies of slate, Durango Pete and I left the house. He was as gay as spring sunshine. He knew what a change in seasons was about. He knew that we were headed someplace new on our walk that day. Well—I told him, of course. But he knew it before I uttered a word. Durango Pete always knows what I am thinking before I know that I am thinking it.

We circled the neighborhood pond on our way to the Hogback. The water rippled in a breeze that was slight but bracing. The path was empty. It was just Pete and I walking past the willows and the homes that ringed the large pond. The Hogback loomed above us to the west, and beyond it—and higher yet—the foothills covered in scrub oak and ponderosa pines were draped with low-hanging clouds and mists. The flakes of snow continued to fall in lazy patterns, drifting downward and in well-spaced intervals. Pete and I had much elbow room that morning, as did the flakes of snow.

The Dakota Hogback is a noteworthy landmark. This is a ridge that runs from northern New Mexico, through Colorado, along the western edge of the plains, to its northern terminus in southern Wyoming. It is named after the Dakota Formation although it is the Fountain Formation that, in fact, underlies the ridge. The ridge was formed around fifty million years ago, which coincided with the formation of the modern Rocky Mountains. In geologic time, many of the rock strata comprising the Hogback are much older. There is much in the way of fossilized evidence to support this. Dinosaur footprints are found there, and they can still be seen on the ridge near Morrison, not far from our house.

Before long, Pete and I left the concrete paths and started up the dirt trail that ran straight through the golden rabbitbrush and the pale green yucca that distinguish the open spaces east of the Hogback. The trail turned hard left, to the south, right before the scrub oak and ponderosa pines appeared. Of course, I talked to Durango Pete the entire time we walked. I have the gift of gab, and to Pete I was pointing out this feature of the landscape and that species of flora. The fauna had been shy thus far. We saw no animals.

I wore my favorite pair of jeans, a comfortable zip turtleneck shirt, a vest, and my Gore-Tex shell. Pete wore his natural sweater of cream fur, dotted with closely spaced chocolate spots. We were both dressed just right.

As Pete and I entered the thick scrub of Gambel oaks, the trail tilted up sharply, and we negotiated our first rock ledges. Much of the rock was crumbly. I am less sure-footed than I used to be, and Pete had been very good on the leash thus far. I didn't want Pete to pull me off-balance, and I wanted him to have some free time off the leash. He did ask for—OK, demand—a treat every thirty yards or so. We had trained him well. With a smile on my face, I silently cursed Tim the Trainer. I called Pete over and unhooked the leash from his collar. He smiled, and then he was gone, leaping up the ledges ahead of me. I grinned from ear to ear to see his dog joy and his skills at rock climbing. I lumbered along behind.

When Durango Pete got too far ahead, I hollered, "Pete—wait!" He did. I was happy and relieved beyond measure that he was cooperating. Of course, he asked for, and got, another treat as a reward.

After a half-hour of walking and climbing, Pete and I reached the saddle that split the spine of the Hogback. We had not seen a human soul. We had not seen any deer or coyotes either, even though they are common on the Hogback. I kept a keen eye out for mountain lions and for their tracks and scat. We were in their habitat.

To the west, the Hogback dropped off into a broad valley a half-mile in width. Beyond the valley, the real mountains began, rising to loom over us, the summits eight hundred to a thousand feet above Pete and me.

Pete scampered here and there. There was plenty of good sniffing to be had. I walked along behind him in quiet reflection. Now and then, in some seemingly arbitrary spot on the trail, a green thing held forth. I wondered what circumstances allowed a few plants to maintain their summer foliage when almost all the others had succumbed to the colder temperatures and the shortened days. Were those that held on simply hardier than the rest? Had they, through serendipity, found the few places on the trail that were protected from the cold winds and that allowed enough sun to be captured and the coursing of chlorophyll to continue despite the season? How had they been the lucky ones to escape the crush of dusty boots like mine on the trail? There was a metaphor here.

I looked up from my cerebral wanderings to check on Pete. He remained close by, and he appeared to be altogether engrossed in his own reverie. I went back to my walking and wondering.

Still looking for plants that were survivors, I thought about my own people: my ancestors who had walked these very foothills and low mountains looking for gold and silver. Porter Timothy Hinman was the first of my people to arrive in the Colorado Territory. The year was 1860. He was my great-grandfather, removed three times. He had been on his own since the tender age of fifteen, when both his father and mother had been swept away in a cholera outbreak in New York.

Porter T. was experienced in a lot of things, practical and otherwise. He was a clerk on a steamship that plied the Great Lakes. He was a teacher of writing and English. He was a farmer, a sawmill owner, a postal clerk, and a miner. Most of all, he was a wanderer, a dreamer, and an optimist. Along the way, he married a pretty, and smart, girl from Coshocton, Ohio. Her name was Mary Platt Smith, and she and Porter T. Hinman had seven children.

Before he came to Colorado, Porter T. had been to California—part of the rush of humanity eager for adventure and riches in 1849 that was the California Gold Rush. It was there that he learned the hard work and lessons of gold mining. When his prospecting proved unfruitful, he started a freighting company that provided income and enough cash to return to Iowa two years later. His family awaited his coming home.

He lasted eight years as a mill owner and postal clerk In Polk County, Iowa, before the itch began again. Gold had been discovered on Cherry Creek in Colorado. In 1860, Porter T. and his two oldest sons, Porter Mortimer and Platt, arrived on Left Hand Creek in Boulder Valley. There they homesteaded 320 acres of land.

As the years went by, both good fortune and tragedy befell Porter T.'s children. Porter M., his oldest son, was dead at the age of forty from a morphine overdose he had self-administered for his debilitating neuralgia. B.T. died as an infant, a horrible death from scarlet fever. Merritt (my great-great-great-grandfather) committed suicide in a Leadville boarding house, destitute and recently divorced. The divorce papers were found in his breast pocket. He was only forty-two years old. Homer, the middle child (like me), lived a long life, eventually settling in the Pacific Northwest, where he passed away at the age of eighty-five. The youngest of Porter T.'s children, Frank Arnold, became a rich mine owner near Steamboat Springs, Colorado. Frank was also a saloon owner, and he was a rancher on the Little Snake River near the Wyoming-Colorado border. But he too died young, in Tincup, Colorado, at only forty-three years old. The only daughter, Augusta, married Jeremiah Leggett in 1861. They became prominent ranchers near Boulder, and she lived until she was eighty-seven years old. Porter T. outlived many of his children. He died an old man on Frank Arnold's ranch on the Little Snake River in 1900. Porter T. was eighty-four years old.

I thought how we were like the plants. Some died early and easily—some early and hard. Others, though, survived. And some thrived and blossomed and propagated their own progeny, who began the cycle of success and suffering again. I thought about those who were even older than my people, those who hunted and camped where I was then walking on the Hogback with Durango Pete. They had been no different. They had experienced the same hardships and serendipities. They had experienced them thousands of years earlier, not 157 years, as my people had. My existential journey ended abruptly when Durango Pete tapped me on my knee with his nose. He was hungry. I was his Pez dispenser.

Eventually, Pete and I made it home from the Hogback, unscathed by mountain lions, bears, or snakes. We
had shared an outing in the wild. He had been allowed
to be a dog in the elemental sense, unchained and free
to go where his powerful nose and his reptilian brain led
him. I was given the gift of being in nature, a place much
more suited to my soul than a desk in our house or a concrete path in our neighborhood. There is a door that is
opened by the simple, repetitive act of putting one foot in
front of the other on a dusty, winding path in the hills. The
rhythm of boots striking soil, the swinging of arms, and
the elemental focus of eyes searching the path quiet the
persistent noise of living and thinking and worrying. I had
been freed to allow my mind to quiet until the sounds of
boots scuffing dirt, birds singing, the rustle of Pete brush-
ing the grasses and oaks, and the silence—most of all the
silence—soothed my soul and took me places. I traveled
far beyond the Hogback on that day. A simple walk in the
wilds allowed me to touch my very being. I am certain that
Pete had done the same. The best part of the day was that
we had traveled together, as partners on the trail.

That day was the beginning of a "muttual" understanding. It was truly the start of the best parts of the adventure that is our life with Pete. Pete has stimulated many
reflections about life on my part. And as a result, he has
allowed me to discover a whole spiritual and philosophical
side of myself that had been submerged for at least forty-
five years as I was immersed in careers and starting and
raising a family. As I like to say, "At the age of five, I was
fully connected with the Creator. At the age of sixty-six, I
am slowly working my way back." The more that Durango

Pete and I hit the trails and wild spaces in Colorado and elsewhere, the more we became connected and the more I reconnected to that which is divine, the essence. Durango Pete pointed me down the trail to sights and sounds and epiphanies that would have remained undiscovered without him. I showed him lots of places and things too.

My struggle with Durango Pete was not unique. It happens every day, in our family relationships, in our work relationships, and in our relationships with perfect strangers and friends. It is really a struggle for power. I had been working to make Pete what I envisioned he should be—my ideal. This happens all the time. We want to fix somebody. We want to change that person into whom we want them to be, which most often has nothing to do with what they envision or who they are on the most basic level. It should be no surprise, then, that a person—or a dog—might not like that. He or she might not cooperate. And, even if we win the struggle for dominance or power, even if we succeed in achieving their acquiescence, it will not be willingly on that person or animal's part, nor will it be out of respect or love. It will be out of fear. The alpha roll episodes with Durango Pete were emblematic. Someone is always harmed when alpha rolled, dog or person. It had been an intuitive response that I had when I alpha rolled Pete. I knew that it was opposite of everything my very soul instructed me that was right for me and for Pete. I knew that this was a bad technique and that it was harming Pete and it was harming me. In the end, it was harming our relationship. I had turned loose of the alpha roll, and at that point, I was turning loose of other things that were harming Durango Pete and me.

Durango Pete had to have some freedom to be who he was. He needed to express who he was when he came into this world. There was a wild side to him that I was learning to respect. His intellect had to be used in ways that were not destructive but that still allowed him the chance to display and challenge it. His ancient genetic characteristics and drive had to be given freedom to manifest. Finally, he had to be allowed to receive affection and to give affection—in ways that were natural and right for him. The animal communicator told me that Pete and I were meant to be together. She told me that Pete would allow me to use and grow my natural skills. None of this meant that there could be no rules or expectations for certain behaviors. Any good relationship is a partnership. It is an unfolding of ongoing give and take and compromise—and some sacrifices. The animal communicator, after all, had told me that Pete was with me to learn how to live in the bourgeois world of humans and cities and streets and shops and grandchildren and expectations and—yes—even some rules.

In the end, I decided that Durango Pete and I were going to develop a partnership—the best partnership we could. I was going to listen to him. I hoped that he was going to listen to me. I committed to giving him what he needed, and I believed that he would give me something to be treasured: a friendship and companionship that transcended our differences as human and dog.

I thought about the plants on the Hogback trail that had survived into late fall. I thought about the ones that were gone and about the new ones that would appear the following spring. Where would they find purchase? How long would they shine? I thought about my people—the old Colorado Hinmans. They had come into the world as unique living organisms. They put feet to their own paths, not knowing for certain where they would end up or how long their lights would shine on the earth. I know that they struggled, and they sometimes failed and sometimes succeeded. I know that there were relationships they experienced that thrived and those that shriveled and died. I thought about my own life. I had already surpassed many of my ancestors in age. I had no idea when or where my journey would end. I had no true idea how many years Durango Pete would have to explore and play and sniff things at home or in the wilderness. These things are not ours to know. But the time we are given is ours to make the best of. I knew that the best things in life revolve around relationships. Whatever time Pete and I had together—well, I wanted it to be the best possible. I wanted to share those times as sentient beings on equal footing. He could teach me. I would teach him. Where and when it ended was out of my hands and Pete's paws. It was time for us to really begin our adventure together. And Colorado and the American West were going to be great places for the two of us to roam.

PART TWO

ADVENTURES & LESSONS

INTRODUCTION

DURANGO PETE WAS FOUR OR five months old when our adventures began in the natural places in Colorado and the great American West. The groundwork had been laid. That day in December, our first big outing on the Hogback had whetted my appetite for wandering in the wild places, as I had done as a boy. Durango Pete was eager too. We were discovering a kinship of our own lives—a mutual love of nature, the great outdoors, and sharing our insights with each other. We were both getting the exercise we needed. We both discovered new places and saw sights that were unexpected and joyful to see. The trails and paths we walked became trips of self-discovery, of education about history and the unfolding of a relationship deep and beautiful. How could I have known what an adventure life with Durango Pete would be!

One day out on the trail, Durango Pete and I were walking and talking (as we do). Pete said to me, "Dad, life is a series of events and choices—the outcomes of which are largely unknown."

It was spring, I think. I thought about what he said. I replied, "You are right, Pete. The bud opens when the time is right. Spring cannot be hurried."

Pete and I learn something every time we hit the trails. The best trips are always the ones that are unforced, the ones where Pete and I simply let a walk unfold. Expectations are best left behind. Stuff often happens when we do that—mostly good stuff. Even the bad things we occasionally experience become useful and instructive.

When my mind is quiet, Pete speaks to me—when he has something to say or when I have a question to ask him. Often, Pete simply makes an observation, and that idea appears in my head. There is never any doubt about its origin. Durango Pete is both a funny dog and a deep dog. He is a poet and a cow dog philosofur. Sometimes, I make an observation. I share it with Pete. On the most special days, a "musing" about life or the seeds for a poem sprout. Pete cannot use a keyboard. So, upon our return home, it is my job to write down or compose the completed version of the prose and poetry that were given birth on our adventure. The titles of each chapter in Part Two are examples of these musings. Many chapters include poems that were written thanks to that adventure.

Durango Pete and I hope you enjoy a few of our tales, the people we met, and the history of the places we rambled. Perhaps our musings, philosophical wanderings, and poetry will pluck a string for you and help your own bud to bloom. Lace up your boots, quiet your minds, and join us for a bit of fun, philosophy, history, and poetry on the dusty trails.

CHAPTER 7

"Those Who Make Little Tracks Are No Less Significant Than Those Who Howl at the Moon."

Mr. Steve and Durango L. Pete

I AM A HOPELESS WANDERER. It is how I came into this world. There is no "fixing it"—except to get my daily dose of being outside, putting my feet to a path under the expanse of the sky, winding through cottonwoods, scrub oaks, willows, and aspens, and listening to the sounds of that day's wilderness. Even if it is simply the patches of wilderness found in the midst of cities and suburbs, I need that dose. I expected that Durango Pete would be the same, a wanderer and explorer. He is a cattle dog, after all.

Cynthia, Pete, and I are fortunate to live in a small suburb of Denver on the very southwest-most boundary of the metropolis. Within five miles of our house, we have an amazing array of open spaces, state parks, mountain parks, canyons, rivers, lakes, and trails to explore and enjoy. Of course, Durango Pete has the same opportunities when he wanders with us. We live in Colorado, a state that abounds in natural beauty of a diversity that is breathtaking. We are not shy about taking advantage of the wilderness and outdoor spaces that the state affords. It was time to give Durango Pete a proper introduction to his new home state.

One day in January of 2013, when Durango Pete was five and a half months old, he and I headed out for a new adventure not far from home. We had to drive there in our car; we call it the *adventure mobile*. We made our usual stop at Sonic to get a breakfast burrito—egg and cheese only—and a cup of coffee. Pete loves Sonic. He gets burrito bites for breakfast when we do a morning stop. He gets a plain hot dog when we stop after a ramble. If I say the word "Sonic," Pete's ears spring straight up. Anyhow, we stopped at Sonic for a breakfast burrito on the way to our morning ramble. I wasn't sure where we were going to hike. But most of the trails were north of our house, so I headed that way.

Sometimes, when I can't make up my mind where to go for a ramble, I ask Pete what we should do for our hike. Or I throw it out to the Universe. That morning, Pete didn't answer when I asked him where we should go. So I tossed the question out to the Universe. The Universe answered. The Universe told me to bypass Chatfield State Park near our home. So I did. The Universe said to turn left at Deer Creek Canyon Road. So I did. We passed Cathy Johnson Open Space. The Cathy Johnson trail looked inviting, but the Universe didn't give me the go-ahead to ramble there. Next, we passed the trailhead at South Valley Park. "Nope!" the Universe said.

Up the canyon we went. The Universe told me to turn left at Deer Creek Park. I did. Pete was along for the ride.

We wound back and forth, up the twisting, steep road into Deer Creek Park. We passed the Rattlesnake Gulch Trail and the red rock outcroppings that mark its path. We passed the first few multi-million dollar homes that dot the benchland between the Hogback to the east and the rising pine-covered mountains to the west. We turned into the parking lot at Deer Creek Park. We did as the Universe instructed. There were only two cars in the parking lot. The Universe must be right, I thought.

The trail that the Universe told me to walk on that day was a Front Range trail, meaning that the trail was located in a transition zone between the high prairie, upon which Denver and its suburbs sit, and the first mountain range that arises from the prairie. On our way to the trailhead, we passed through the Dakota Hogback geological formation. As you know, Pete and I simply call the long ridge (and paired ridges in some sections) "the Hogback." The parking lot Pete and I pulled into sat just west of the Hogback and just east of the first mountain range.

Durango Pete was eager to escape the car. It was a sunny day. There was a slight breeze, and the temperature was warm enough that I only needed a shell jacket and a light vest underneath. It had snowed a few days before, so I knew that the lower trail, which traveled up the gully, would still be muddy. The Universe told me to take Meadowlark Trail instead. I followed the command of the great Universe.

Pete was on his leash. Deer Creek Park is an on-leash trail. He wasn't happy about being tethered. But I told him that we are all tethered in some fashion. The Universe smiled and acknowledged this observation. Even though we don't often ramble at Deer Creek, Durango Pete knows the trail, and he has a routine that is always followed.

There are great numbers of yucca and rabbitbrush that dot the open landscape at the start of the trail. These, Durango Pete felt, must be properly sniffed. So our initial progress was slow. Allowing Pete ample time to use his olfactory powers was part of the bargain I had recently made. There is a good amount of leg-lifting and peeing that must be done too. One bodily function often leads to the next. Soon Pete was taking care of his second order of business in the choice spot that he had selected. The Universe must have spoken to him as well.

The trail soon left the park-like landscape and entered the first stands of woody scrub oak. I enjoyed walking through the shady tunnel of trees. It is home to scrub jays and chickadees, and I spotted a few unfamiliar birds as well. I kept an eye out for interesting rocks along the way. Sometimes they do speak to you. Durango Pete scampered left and right, making sure to explore every inch of the path and the apron of the trail on each side. Walking Durango Pete on his leash is interval training of sorts. We move briskly along for twenty yards—then stop. Onward we travel in this halting fashion. It is a schizophrenic workout for my heart. I think a dog's heart is designed—by the Universe, of course—with this erratic pattern and behavior in mind. A toss of a treat now and then helped our forward advancement (thank you, Tim the Trainer). Pete was making progress with his leash walking.

We passed Rattlesnake Corner (where a few years later, Pete, Cynthia, and I were forced to turn around by a cantankerous prairie rattler in the middle of the trail), and we started up the series of switchbacks that climb the lower slopes of the first mountains. My breathing deepened. My heart rate picked up pace too, and soon I was stripping off my waterproof, lightweight shell. We paused to look at the view that spread out below us, to the north, east, and south. It was a glorious sight. I could see all the way to Green Mountain northeast of us. Green Mountain is only green for a short time in the spring, when there has been ample moisture and moderate temperatures. The rest of the time it is either white (which it was at the time), dusted in snow, or golden or tan, the predominant colors as the grass and vegetation crisp in the dry air and warmth of the sun in summer and fall.

After we completed the six switchbacks, Pete and I crossed over to the west side of the first mountain, where it dropped off precipitously to the west. I always get a touch of vertigo there. It is kind of exhilarating. Durango Pete wandered to the edge and perched proudly on the spot where the exposure was greatest. There he stood, seemingly oblivious to the danger, and he looked into the distance with his ears on full alert and his brown nose twitching in the breeze. When the Universe speaks, a dog listens. I decided it was a good time for me to prick my ears, turn my nose to the wind, and listen to the Universe and the old voices too. As I stood there with Pete, a poem came to me.

Now I Am

By Stephen Hinman & Durango L. Pete

In old age, I am reconnected to my ancient self
The one that hears the voices
Of the Earth, the Sky, and the Eagle.

I now see
Molecules moving air.
I now hear
The cry of the cold snow beneath my feet.
I now feel
The brush of the breeze rolling up my rough neck
The scuff of the scrub oak against my jeans
The warmth of the granite where I sit to rest.
I now smell
The earth damp with Heaven's tears shed
The grass pungent and sweet
The pines that tickle my nose with fresh delight.
I am, now.
Now, I am.

After I spent some time standing there with Pete and
jotting down a draft of my poem on my cell phone, we
began walking again. I decided to look for signs of spring.
It was far too early. But a man can always hope. I am nothing if not an optimist. I tried to remember the late winter
months and the spring as a boy growing up in Colorado.

Back then, in the 1950s and 1960s, I was busy playing baseball. Every recollection I could conjure about spring back then was filtered through the yearly rituals associated with the great American pastime, a sport in which I had been eagerly and fully engaged.

During the spring as a boy, I spent only a little time wandering the fields and open land that surrounded Denver's infant suburbia. Everything outdoors, for me, revolved around an acre of grass and dirt surrounded by chain link fences and tall backstops. I remembered March as an enormously exasperating month. My teammates and I were wildly hopeful that the necessary routines of shagging balls in the outfield and working on footwork and the proper position for fielding grounders would take place in the fresh air outdoors. Mother Nature was usually a tease and often did not cooperate. We spent many practices in the smelly confines of the school gymnasium, fielding scorching ground balls that screamed across varnished hardwood floors, hit sharply with the coach's long, skinny fungo bat.

On that day with Durango Pete, I didn't know what signs of the brightening, hopeful days ahead I would find hiking a mountain trail in late January. I examined the ground as Pete I wandered up the trail, looking for green sprouts poking tentative heads through the earth still moist from the recent snows and warmed by an unusually strong January sun. I didn't have much success finding signs of rebirth and new life. I was growing weary of winter. I was as impatient with winter then as I was when I was a ballplayer at the age of sixteen. I envied Durango Pete. He clearly was not worried about when winter would end and when spring might or might not arrive. There was plenty of fine sniffing, looking, and peeing to be done right then, just as things were. Ha! As the poem said: *I am, now. Now, I am.* Clearly, there was much that I might learn from Durango Pete. I quieted my impatient mind and focused on my footsteps.

Durango Pete and I reached the upper part of the trail, where it leveled out as it traversed the eastern flank of the mountain before swinging right and to the west. As we moved into the shadier section of the trail, it became muddy. I wasn't eager to muck my way through the heavy, wet red clay. Pete and I turned around and headed back down. It was going to be a shorter ramble than I had hoped. I figured that the Universe was looking out for us. Perhaps some pitfall awaited us if we had forged on through the mud. It is best to trust the Universe. The Universe knows best.

As we descended, I was lost in reverie, and Durango Pete was busy in his own world closer to the ground and about seven feet ahead of me on his leash. I didn't see the trail runner, an elderly man in his early seventies, until he was nearly on top of us. I tried to reel Pete in by his retractable leash, hoping that the runner would stop until I could get Pete next to me. But runners are often loath to stop running. I see them jogging in place at stoplights or stop signs, as if their workout is negated if their legs do not move continually from start to finish. This old man was heading right for us on a trail that was only two feet wide and where I struggled with my cattle dog, still on a too-long lead.

The old runner looked cartoonish, as elderly runners often do. He was dressed all in black. He wore a tight-fitting long-sleeved top. The form-fitting Lycra revealed a paunch that jiggled as he ran. His black running shorts were "old school," too short for a man of his age. They rode high on his waist and made his skinny red legs look longer than they were. His naked legs were the color of beets from the cool temperatures and exertion. He looked like a stork moving up the trail. He had a thick shock of white hair, parted on one side, and a white mustache that hung down at each corner of his mouth. His lips were thin and turned downward in a scowl. He had ice-blue eyes that were piercing, and they peered out from behind squinty, hooded lids. He looked familiar. I was sure that I had seen him on the trail before.

Durango Pete is rarely disagreeable to humans he meets on the path. But he is often exuberant. He is a wild-looking hound, with his stick-up ears, his wolf-like yellow eyes, and his powerful neck and shoulders. Had I been the stranger approaching Pete on the path, I would have stopped to allow the dog's owner to gain close control—or to ask the owner if the dog was friendly. The gray-haired runner did neither. He forged ahead, leaning forward and grinding up the path. Clearly his running was slow-but-serious business. As he passed us, Durango Pete jumped up to greet him. The man backhanded Pete across the nose and yelled at him, "Get off!" Pete was knocked backward by the blow. I was stunned.

I shouldn't have been surprised. I realized that Durango Pete and I had encountered this man several other times at Deer Creek Park. I make a point of saying hello to all I meet on the trail. Sometimes, the passerby responds in a friendly fashion. Sometimes there is no acknowledgment. Often, I know what the response to my salutation will be, even before it takes place. I have an ability to identify the aura possessed by most people I encounter. This elderly fellow was not possessed of a glowing aura of friendliness. He had never reciprocated my greetings before. So, I should not have been surprised by his response to Durango's friendly but forward greeting, but I was. In fact, I was not only surprised, I was angry when he hit Pete in the snout. I said something to the old dude—probably asking if that had really been necessary. I hope I did not include a sailor's expression or two in my response. But I cannot guarantee that I did not.

The man stopped and turned around. "You need to teach your dog some damn manners—or get him under goddamned control!" he yelled. He was red in the face and leaning forward, with his fists balled up at his sides.

I replied, "This trail allows dogs. If you are going to run here, you better get used to seeing dogs on the trail." Then, I added, "We have a right to be here too!" Finally, I may have concluded my response with "You miserable SOB!" I am not sure about the last part. If I did say it, I guess the Universe was to blame. After all, I could have just as easily rambled at Chatfield or Cathy Johnson Open Space that day. Durango Pete and I had simply followed the wishes of the Universe. I have come to suspect that the Universe often has a lesson it wants to teach Durango Pete and me. I think the Universe wants us to experience the Yin in life, not only the Yang.

I was "out of sorts" following our encounter with the trail-running curmudgeon. I fumed about the sad state of humanity the entire trip down the mountain. Spring could have been "springing" all around me and I would have noticed none of it. Durango Pete seemed unfazed by the whole ordeal. He continued to go about his dog business of sniffing and peeing and pausing to look at stuff. I needed to be more like Pete. Hell, we all needed to be more like Durango Pete—especially the old man with the scowl, who was still back up the trail, running on the mountain with his skinny, red legs that looked like a stork's. Clearly, though, I was getting attached to our little cattle dog. I didn't like someone swatting him across his nose! I would keep Pete on a shorter lead at Deer Creek, but I would look after Pete too. Would he look after me?

I stopped at Sonic on the way home. Even though our ramble had been abbreviated and we didn't do enough walking to expend many calories, the disturbing ordeal warranted a hot dog and ice cream, in my estimation. Durango Pete didn't argue. I didn't ask the Universe for permission. I simply stopped—for a bit of comfort food for Pete and me.

Later that day, Durango Pete and I headed back out for another ramble. I decided to stay close to home. The Universe had gone quiet. So it was up to me to pick a location for our afternoon outing. I figured that Pete and I could walk from our house to the Highline Canal Trail and then onward to the south-side Chatfield trails. We typically see few people once we reach the Highline and Chatfield. I was not much interested in additional encounters with humans.

Pete and I walked along in silence. Before I knew it, we had covered three miles, and we were crossing the sagebrush and yucca prairie on the south side of Chatfield State Park. We were alone. The sun had disappeared, and the sky had turned the color of the dark-blue steel on a rifle barrel. Low, angry-looking clouds draped the tops of the peaks to the west as we walked. The weather and the experience earlier in the day conspired to turn my mood dark. I shuffled along under the stormy skies, kicking stones and dirt as I went. Once in a while, I gave a stone an extra hard boot, pretending it was the old runner at Deer Creek. I didn't see any signs of life, not even a bug.

The Universe works in mysterious ways. As I was feeling lower than a dusty old sandbur, a flock of bluebirds skimmed the tops of the brush directly in our path. There must have been fifty of them flying in low, tight formation, creating a flash of dazzling sapphire. They sailed along above the buff-colored prairie. Pete was already at attention, watching the bluebirds playing in the wind. I stopped to watch too. Durango Pete and I smiled. Yes, the Universe often makes things right again, even sending bluebirds to metaphorically land on my shoulder. I said "thank you" to the bluebirds and to the Universe. I was happy to welcome the return of the Yang. I tucked the Yin away and closed the sour drawer for the time being.

For Durango Pete, life appeared to be one giant Yang. He didn't seem to possess a "sour drawer." I promised myself that I would work on being more like Durango Pete and less like the miserable old man who smacked an exuberant cattle dog on the nose. Many of us humans scream at the wind, and we can cause such a ruckus and heartbreak all on our own without any help. Some people think a dog is not as worthy as we are. It's "only" an animal, after all. But, like the people who carry on their own quiet lives with charity and kindness and without bluster, a little dog who is simply happy to meet someone on the trail is no less important than those who howl at the moon. I was discovering that my connection with Pete was growing stronger. And I was finding out that a small cow dog can have big mojo.

CHAPTER 8

"Sometimes We Need to Stop Moving to Know Where We Are."

Mr. Steve & Durango L. Pete

L IFE WITH DURANGO PETE WAS a whirlwind. I suppose that becoming a cattle dog owner at sixty-two years of age has an upside. Without Pete and his demands for exercise and stimulation, I could easily have adopted the doting lifestyle that often accompanies one's senior years. I like to say, "Durango Pete will either save me, or he will kill me." Which of the two remains to be seen. I do a lot of moving with Durango Pete; that is for sure. But Pete has taught me to stop too. When I listen to him, and I take a pause on the trail, or when we sit on a rock in the wilderness for a while, I receive a gift. Sometimes we do need to stop moving. And in the stillness we find things that, long ago, we knew.

One lazy weekday morning in the month of February, I still lay in bed with Durango Pete while Cynthia was already up and at her workstation in our house. I felt guilty lounging while she was already working. Pete had no compunction about stretching out in sleepy bliss on her side of the bed when she was gone.

I reached down and gave him a good scritch on his head and removed some sleep from his eyes. "Well, Pete, what do you want to do today?"

"Anything but another neighborhood walk or pond loop!" he told me.

OK, then. I figured it was a good day for a trip up to a section of the Hogback a few miles north of our house and to the Cathy Johnson Trail that parallels the base of the Hogback. Durango Pete and I love the Hogback trails and even bushwhacking the brush and rock outcroppings that are unique to its landscapes. We see wonderful things there. And we often have spiritual, mysterious experiences.

Three significant rivers or creeks cut through the Hogback near our home: the South Platte River, Deer Creek, and Bear Creek. The protection provided by the sandstone formations located near the Hogback, the presence of water, and the abundance of game made the Hogback an attractive camping and hunting area for the Native American tribes who populated the Front Range in Colorado and for the Paleo-Indians who came before them. Artifacts can still be found near the Hogback, and many have been removed as part of archaeological expeditions and digs that took place after the area was settled by European Americans. I have great reverence for the history of the area and for the people, families, and cultures who called the Hogback home long before Durango Pete and me.

I am particularly drawn to the spirituality of the first tribes that called the Rocky Mountains their home. I attended Bible school and church when I was a boy. I have been an irregular attendee as an adult. As I have aged, my spirituality has gotten more complicated in some respects, yet much simpler in the net. Just as Durango Pete is a cattle dog mix, I am a mutt ancestrally and spiritually. Despite my Presbyterian upbringing, there is much about Native American spirituality that resonates with me, especially their reverence for the natural world and the gifts that animals and birds and grasses and trees bestow upon us. My Native American totem is the wolf. It seems fitting.

The wolf symbolizes a deep understanding and connection with natural instincts. A person with a wolf totem or spirit animal has a bond with the natural world, and while there is an awareness of the importance of social connections, there can be a wariness. Trust must be earned. The wolf is a pathfinder and ventures deep into the wilderness to find sustenance. All of this resonates with me and is immediately recognizable as part of my personality. I think this is part of why Durango Pete and I battled so hard and why there is a connection between us at a deep level.

As I said, Durango Pete and I have had strange experiences while walking in the Hogback. Pete and I hike there more than any other place in Colorado. It is where Pete and I saw a huge coyote one winter day a few years later. The coyote appeared out of nowhere. The snow was drifting down in huge wet flakes. The clouds were low, and the Hogback was draped in mists and fog that scooted along the ridge and the Hogback flanks. The coyote walked slowly out of the fog. He was fantastic—as big as a wolf. In fact, I was not sure that it wasn't a wolf and not a coyote, even though wolves have been gone from Colorado for years. I turned to Pete to see if he had spotted the coyote. When I turned back, the coyote was gone. I felt his yellow eyes on me the remainder of our hike that day, and I often looked over my shoulder to see if he was there. Later that night, Pete and I wrote a poem about the coyote.

The Coyote

By Stephen Hinman & Durango L. Pete

The coyote wanders through the yucca

Lazy

Until the craziness comes crashing

Up

And he leaps.

Pete and I have some other great memories of our walks on the Hogback that we want to tell you before we get to the story that is the main subject of this chapter. Pardon us while we digress.

The Hogback is prime habitat for raptors. Pete and I have seen bald eagles, red-tailed hawks, goshawks, prairie falcons, and golden eagles on our many hikes up and down the valley and during our rambles on the flanks and spines of the Hogback. The eagles are particularly mysterious. They appear when we least expect them. If Durango Pete and I talk about looking for them and I say, "Pete, I sure hope we will see eagles today," we never are graced with their appearance. They show up when we are quiet and deep in thought and engrossed in the simple act of moving forward. That is when they suddenly appear. They often disappear just as quickly. Rarely do they linger or play in the thermals long enough for us to watch them for any significant duration. A pair of mating bald eagles is especially exciting for Durango and me to see although we see them the least frequently of all the birds of prey in the valley.

One day, a year after that morning when Pete and I still lay in bed, working up the willpower and energy to arise and begin the day, Durango Pete and I adventured on the Hogback near the Cathy Johnson Trail. It was a spring day, as I recall. Durango Pete was a year and a half old at the time.

We were returning to the trailhead after a long ramble up the valley between two ridges, one of which, on the east side of the valley, is called the Dakota Hogback, and the second ridge which skirts the west side of the valley and is called the Lyons Hogback.

It was a sunny, cold, day with a brilliant blue sky and few clouds. Durango Pete suddenly stopped and sat down, looking left. I have learned to pay attention to Pete when he puts on the brakes. Usually he has spotted or heard something that he wants to check out. Movement caught my eye high above the eastern ridge. I could see two birds circling above the highest cliff band on the spine. One of the two birds was large, an obvious fact even though Pete and I were a long distance away. I was sure that the larger bird must be a golden eagle because of the wingspan and size and color. The other bird was a third the size of the eagle. Suddenly the eagle made a run at the smaller bird and collided with it in midair! The smaller bird tumbled for a bit, falling lower and lower after the collision. I could see its white- or light-colored breast as it fell. It recovered after dropping a few hundred feet, and it hightailed it out of there, not wanting to suffer another attack by the eagle. The large, copper-colored eagle disappeared to the south. It was an amazing sight to see. Durango Pete and I looked at each other as if to say, "Wow! Did you see that?" I thanked Pete for stopping us on the trail that day and for the vision we experienced. A few eagle poems have been penned by Durango Pete and me. We wrote the following poem during a rest stop on a large sandstone rock that very day.

Eagle Visions

By Stephen Hinman & Durango L. Pete

The eagle appears
Floating
My blood rushes.
Then it vanishes
Always
I am left alone wondering.

The eagle is a powerful totem and spirit guide in Native American culture and spirituality. The Arapaho, who lived and hunted in the Hogback, considered the appearance of an eagle to be a positive sign. They believed that the eagle was a messenger from the creator. They believed the eagle could travel between man and the creator.

The eagle was also important to the Utes, who frequented the area near the Hogback to hunt. Pete and I have no doubts that the tribes who walked and rode over the same landscape we traveled had their own eagle encounters and their own eagle visions. The Southern Ute Cultural Center & Museum, located in Ignacio, Colorado, is built in the shape of an eagle. For me, the appearance of an eagle affirms the connections that Durango Pete and I have with a higher power. Eagle medicine and dog medicine are good medicines for sure.

Hawks are much more common on our rambles on and near the Hogback. The most common hawk we see is the red-tailed hawk. But we have also seen goshawks, Swainson's hawks and rough-legged hawks. On another ramble up the valley floor on the Cathy Johnson Trail, between ridges, Durango Pete and I stopped to marvel at a rough-legged hawk that was hovering like a helicopter at the edge of the eastern ridge. It was a breezy day, and the updraft and thermals flowing up the west-facing cliff bands must have been very strong. We stopped and watched the hawk hover for five minutes. Durango Pete told me that he wanted to do that—like the hawk we were watching. I understood. When I was a boy, one of my recurring and favorite dreams was that I could fly. I wondered if there were any glider pilots who would let Durango Pete tag along on a flight? I promised myself and Pete to look into that. Good old Durango Pete. He is up for almost anything— that wild, crazy rodeo cowboy.

Sometimes the strange encounters we experience while walking the Hogbacks and the valley between them, don't involve the sighting of coyotes or birds or deer. Sometimes, we hear voices. Bear with us—we aren't delusional. One such experience, perhaps the most profound Pete and I have had while rambling in this place, happened on that sleepy, lazy February morning when Pete and I lounged in bed while Cynthia worked and then decided to go to the Cathy Johnson Trail for our adventure that day.

Pete and I gathered up our usual gear for a Hogback ramble: treat pack, snack crackers, water bottles, and a collapsible dish, refuse bags, sunglasses, camera, phone, and hard candies. Cynthia was still hard at work at her desk. We gave her a kiss. Well, at least I did. Pete was still working on his smooching skills. After the kiss goodbye, off we went in the car. In short order, we arrived at the trailhead and parked along the canyon road. I donned my gear and then got Pete out of the car. We crossed the canyon road to the trailhead.

Cathy Johnson Trail is named after the woman who worked to preserve the open space south of Ken Caryl Ranch. She believed conserving the landscape would benefit the wildlife and plants that inhabit the area and that it was important for us, the public, to enjoy the natural gifts it provided. Pete and I paused at the trailhead sign to look for any notices and to give thanks to Ms. Johnson for her vision and for her work to conserve the area.

The main trail is a rough dirt road that runs from south to north, climbing most of the way to its terminus 2.1 miles from the south trailhead. To the east, the landscape rises steeply to the rock escarpments that mark the top of the Dakota Hogback. To the west, the ground rises a bit less severely to the rocky spine of the Lyons Hogback. There are a few side trails that afford opportunities for Pete and me to do loop hikes and to access South Valley Park to the west of the Lyons Hogback. On many weekdays, Pete and

I encounter no other humans. But during rattlesnake season, my eyes are always on the lookout. Coyotes, mountain lions, deer, elk, foxes, and black bears live in the open space too—and in the other parks and mountains close by. Durango often stops on our rambles in the Dakota and Lyons Hogbacks. Sometimes he stops and looks back over his shoulder. It is a bit unsettling because, aside from sniffing and peeing, he is usually on the march. When he stops and looks back or out, I stop and look too. When he looks behind us, it is as if Pete believes someone or something is following us. Sometimes I will spot someone on the trail far below or behind us. Most often, there is nothing there. Or is there?

That February day, the thermometer in the car registered nine degrees above zero. It was a day of low, gray clouds and a coating of frost on all the branches of the scrub oaks and willows. There was no wind, and there were no cars parked at the trailhead and no other people on the trail. It was only Durango Pete, me, and the scraping sound of my boots on the cold earth. We heard no birds singing, no dead leaves rustling on the branches of the oaks, no airplanes flying overhead—only the sweet sound of silence.

We scrambled through the thick oak and up to the top of the westernmost Lyons Hogback, where we could see the valley below running north and south. We saw the brown line of the distant trail snaking its way along the valley floor. On the top, Pete and I sat on a rock and had a snack of crackers and cheese. Pete got the last bite of each cracker I ate. He prefers the cream cheese and chives crackers. I do too.

Soon, it was time to head back down. As we emerged from the thicket of oak that lined the junction of two trails, Durango Pete stopped. His prominent ears stood straight up, and then he sat down. He wasn't sitting in his typical relaxed, cattle dog sidesaddle sit. He was sitting in his "high alert" posture. He looked across the valley toward the base of the tallest west-facing cliffs. I stopped and looked too. Suddenly, I heard a faint buzzing sound in my ears. It was very strange. It was not the buzzing of insects, an airplane, or saw. It was the sound you hear in a large auditorium when many people are talking at the same time. As I listened, the buzzing gradually became less amorphous. It was the sound of voices, voices of old people talking—women's voices—and the voices of children playing. Durango Pete and I looked at each other with round eyes. I listened for several minutes until the voices dissolved back into buzzing and the buzzing faded back into the silence of the wilderness.

There was no doubt what Pete and I heard that day. It was the voices of the ancient ones who had made the Hogback their home. They, like all who have lived before us and who appear to have departed, remain. They are only a vibration away. Sometimes, when we allow ourselves the gifts of silence, of stillness, of emptying our heads of the constant dialogue and chatter—the old ones speak to us.

They are gifts, the things we can see and feel and hear when we are alone in nature. Sometimes, I need to stop, to know what it is that is there, right before me. And it is these moments when I experience the most profound gifts that nature and wild spaces offer. The "old ones" are not gone. They are just a whisper away. Of course, Durango

Pete, with his ancient dog wisdom and his sensory advantages, already knew this. The way he always knows what I am thinking before I know I am thinking it. Pete often knows what is out there that is profound, ancient, and so easy for us humans to miss. Durango Pete helped me write a poem later that evening about the experience.

The Land Speaks
by Stephen Hinman & Durango L. Pete

The land speaks, but we are too busy to listen.
The hummingbird whistles and the wind rolls
in whispering waves.
The land sings, but we are deaf to the song.
The insects buzz, busy in the beauty
And the old leaves rattle, rusty and reluctant to part.
The land sighs, sweetly and softly, but we are asleep.
The river is a rhapsody, and the call of the hawk catches
on the clouds that wander high and white.
The land whispers a poem so beautiful it breaks
the bravest heart.
But we are lost in a dream, dull and dangerous, full of
clanging noise and hurry and stuff.
The rhyme is removed.

Thank you, Durango Pete, for teaching me how to stop, how to sit still, how to prick my own ears so that I might find gifts that are before me.

CHAPTER 9

"The Only Things We Truly Own Are Our Choices and Our Behaviors."

Mr. Steve & Durango L. Pete

M OST OF THE THINGS WE think we own are ephemeral. Our houses eventually pass on to someone else, or they tumble down with neglect and time, reclaimed by nature, which endures. A car rusts. Our children grow up and leave home to claim their own lives and their own paths and their own choices. Much of the trouble and heartbreak and tragedy in the world, now and before, stems from man's desire to own things: land, treasures, edifices, fellow humans, and even animals, dogs included. In truth, ownership is a fool's errand. The only thing we truly own are the choices we make and our behaviors—the ways in which we interact with the world and other people.

A small family cabin that my parents had purchased years ago in the town of Grand Lake, Colorado, happens to be ours to use—for the time being. Someone had it before us. Someone will have it after our time using it passes.

Durango Pete had been introduced to the cabin early in his life. He didn't take to it initially. But as time went on, and as he grew larger in size and older in months, he came to love the gift of time spent at the cabin and his occasional life in a small mountain town at the western edge of Rocky Mountain National Park.

There is much that Pete loves to do when we are at the cabin. His day up high usually begins with a walk from the cabin to town. It's not a long trip, but it is filled with opportunities for a dog who is inquisitive and not shy.

Along the way to town, Pete and I keep our eyes open for the town black bears or the town foxes, deer, or, best of all, the town moose. Of course, as is the case with many mountain or beach towns, Grand Lake has no shortage of two-legged denizens of odd dress, appearance, and mannerisms. We keep our eyes peeled for them too. No less than the native flora and fauna, these characters give the town flavor and charm. But in the interest of anonymity, they shall go unnamed.

Three lakes mark the Colorado River Valley from Grand Lake to the town of Granby, which lies at the southern terminus of the valley. Lake Granby is the largest of the three, and it is man-made. Shadow Mountain Reservoir is the next lake up the valley, and it sits between Lake Granby and Grand Lake (for which the town is named). Shadow Mountain Reservoir is connected to Grand Lake by a man-made channel and to Lake Granby by the Colorado River. Grand Lake is the only natural lake (it is the largest natural lake in Colorado) of the three, and its depth is significant. The depth of the lake has been measured at four hundred feet. Divers have reported seeing lake trout monstrous in size.

Pete likes to begin his walk by going to the channel that links Grand Lake and Shadow Mountain Reservoir. We cross the channel using the beautiful wood bridge called Rainbow Bridge (seems appropriate that a dog would like that). On the far side, we always stop to gaze at Mount Baldy, which looms over the lake and the town from its eastern perch. After we have appropriately appreciated the massif of granite and snow, we take a shoreline trail to Point Park for swimming. If it is winter and Grand Lake is well frozen, we walk across the lake to town.

If attitude is any indication, Pete believes Grand Lake is his to own. He walks along with a pronounced swagger, and he makes a point to pee on every four-legged interloper's recent deposit. The act is no less significant than the signs that dot the front yards of the homes and businesses in town, proclaiming the name of the person or family who owns the edifice.

Pete has a standard route through town. He has stops he always makes, people he always visits. The coffee shop The Hub is invariably his first stop. That suits me fine. Heather used to be the owner, and it was always a special day if Heather was in the shop. I get a hug, and Pete gets tons of rub-ups and scratches. Then Pete waits on the wooden porch (much to his chagrin and disgust) while I get our goodies—typically a cranberry scone and a vanilla latte. Pete likes his coffee sweet. He only gets a finger lick or two. The scone is shared more evenly. People and dogs come and go, so there are plenty of opportunities for watching the action.

The next stop is Crabtree Realty. We say hello to Elwin, who owns the business. We say hi to Craig, who works there too. Elwin is the best. He is a long-time Grand Lake resident, honest as they come, and he's knowledgeable about the town, local history, and about pretty much anything you want to discuss. Craig is movie-star handsome and no less pleasant than Elwin. He owns a vintage pickup truck that I am drooling to buy. I need to sell a lot of books, though! Pete behaves himself in the shop—sometimes.

After Elwin's shop, we head to Cascade Books to see if Avis is working. I have a soft spot for bookstores, and Cascade Books is one of my favorites. Avis has written several books about Grand Lake. She knows more about Grand Lake history than Elwin! She handpicks every book that she displays and sells in the store. That means that she has also read every book that she sells. Avis has traveled the world and the United States, so she knows about a lot of people and places—not just Grand Lake, Colorado. Avis used to have two bookstore dogs, Shasta and Sierra, a black-and-white border collie and a brown-and-white border collie. Shasta passed away not long before I wrote this book, but Sierra remains vigilant in Shasta's absence, keeping an eye on customers and dogs that enter the shop to browse and chat. Avis has been very encouraging and helpful to me as a fellow writer. Plus, her smile lights up the room.

Our last stop before sitting on a bench by the lake is the town park. It's big enough to satisfy a cattle dog who is looking for some grass or snow upon which to play or make a bathroom stop. The town library is located there, as is the former Grand Lake Repertory Theater. A beautiful new theater has been built up the street, and the summer shows are first-rate and great fun. There is also a small bandstand for summer music, a playground for kids, and a large covered patio with picnic tables for gatherings and bingo.

Across the street from the park is The Sagebrush BBQ & Grill, one of our favorite spots to eat dinner. Durango Pete always looks into the open-air window in the bar area, looking for friends or jackalopes, ne'er-do-wells, malcontents, marauders, and generally unsavory characters. It is a Wild West town, and Pete considers himself to be a sheriff of sorts. Durango Pete once authored a melodrama about The Sagebrush and a few bad apples who tried to take over the town. The story appears in Pete's Facebook blog at facebook.com/durangopete.

Our final stop is the lake. Summer or winter, we occupy a spot on one of the benches and do some fine staring and thinking about things. Remember, sometimes you need to stop moving to know where you are.

Some places are especially powerful. Grand Lake is one such place. A lot of mojo and juju has been well-earned here. Grand Lake is Colorado's oldest tourist attraction. Durango Pete likes to think he owns Grand Lake, but he and I were simply the most recent visitors. Human activity in Grand Lake can be traced back thousands of years, to prehistoric people, Paleo-Indians, and the Native American tribes of the Ute, Cheyenne, and Arapaho. After them came the white explorers and settlers who were looking for passageways, resources, and riches.

All of them set out to own Grand Lake in some way or fashion. But that kind of ownership, as it always does, eventually proves to be a phantom. None of the things they thought they owned were taken to the grave—only the choices they had made. The desire for ownership of places and things and people often ends badly. I thought about this on one of the early trips Pete and I made to the lake. We sat in our usual spot by the water. I reached down and gave Pete a rub on his back as we sat at our bench. He was content for the time being to lie next to me on the shoreline bench, basking in the sun. I was finding out that thinking I owned Durango Pete had led to many of the conflicts and struggles that had been hallmarks of our early relationship. Sharing our resources, our affections, our unique gifts, and our experiences was proving to be a better path. I had confronted the choices I had made in the first months of our time together: the need to be the alpha, the need to give rewards only in return for acquiescence, even the damaging alpha roll. A new method of relating to Durango Pete was evolving. I was happy for the choice I had made to relinquish ownership—master to slave—and to allow Pete to express his value as a living, breathing gift of God, no less important than me or the trees and mountains at which we stared.

As is the case with many desirable things and landscapes, Grand Lake has been the site of struggles and battles since before history was first recorded there. An archaeologist familiar with the area might confirm evidence of warring peoples that predates the Native American tribes. There is evidence and mythology that confirms the struggles between Native American tribes. There is written history, contemporary with the time, that depicts the battles fought by settlers and miners over resources, riches, and power. In fact, one such struggle for power ended in violence and the death of five men.

In 1883, the town of Grand Lake was still in its infancy, having been founded only four years earlier in 1879 by two brothers, William and Bass Redman. They were rough-and-tumble men, reputed to be quick to the trigger. Another town was growing larger at the same time: Hot Sulphur Springs, which was close by, only twenty-five miles to the southwest. A struggle developed over which town would own the title, prestige, and power of being the county seat. In 1881, a vote took place, and the county seat was moved from Hot Sulphur Springs to Grand Lake. There had been lawsuits and much arguing and fighting over the proposed move. Several mining camps had their own allegiances: Lulu City favored the seat moving to Grand Lake; the Teller camp preferred that the county seat remain in Hot Sulphur Springs. The Redman brothers and the Grand Lake supporters had a surprising ally in Teller's John G. Mills.

A few other men from Hot Sulphur were also aligned with the Redman-Mills-Grand Lake faction. One of these men was Charles W. Royer. Royer was elected Grand County sheriff in 1881, and he appointed Bill Redman as his deputy. Redman was based in Grand Lake.

The head of the group that opposed the Grand Lake faction was E.P. Weber, who managed a mine near Rabbit Ears Pass, far to the northwest but still in the county. Barney Day and Captain T.J. Dean, noteworthy Indian fighters and marksmen, also were part of the Hot Sulphur faction.

Hot tempers and bitterness over the move of the county seat from Hot Sulphur Springs to Grand Lake remained in 1882. An election for a new governor of Colorado was looming, with Henry R. Wolcott and Jerome B. Chaffee as the candidates. E.P. Weber and Capt. Dean (Hot Sulphur Springs supporters) were selected as delegates during a rump convention in Grand Lake and sent to the Republican convention to oppose Henry R. Wolcott for governor. At the convention, Weber verbally attacked John G. Mills, calling him a murderer and declaring that he was a wanted man in Missouri.

Things had gotten so hot between the two factions by 1883 that one of the board members of the county commission resigned, and Weber was named his replacement. Soon Weber and Barney Day hatched a plan to remove the county clerk (Lew W. Pollard) and the treasurer without notifying John. G. Mills, the chairman.

A special meeting was called on July 2, 1883. At dusk a move was made to oust the sheriff, Charles W. Royer, along with Pollard, the treasurer, and a county judge. Public outrage was raised to a fever pitch.

The Fairview House was the most popular hotel in Grand Lake at the time. On July 4, 1883, Weber, Day, Dean, and other people from the Teller faction were staying there. At nine o'clock, twelve to fifteen shots rang out. Most people thought it was holiday fireworks. In fact, Weber had been shot. He was found several hundred yards from the hotel, shot through a lung. Dean was found close by, shot through his hip and forehead and his head badly beaten. Barney Day was found with his head in the lake, shot through the heart. Nearby, in the middle of the road, Mills was found dead. A sack had been placed over his head and a bullet had been fired point-blank into the sack. Weber succumbed to his injuries at midnight. Dean died thirteen days later, on July 17.

It is believed that Sheriff Royer was part of the ambushing gang of men. He is believed to have killed Barney Day, shooting him in the chest, when Day had approached Royer

in the melee, thinking Royer was there to help. Royer committed suicide that August, shooting himself at the Innes
House in Georgetown, Colorado, after confessing his part
in the ambush to Ad Kinney, a liveryman in Georgetown.

Bill Redman, who had been wounded and was one of
the attackers, fled to a cabin near Grand Lake and then to
the Flat Tops west of Grand Lake and eventually to Utah,
helped by his brother, Bass Redman.

Another suspect, Alonso Coffin, was tried and acquitted in Golden, Colorado. Other men were also tried and
acquitted. The county seat was moved back to Hot Sulphur
Springs in 1888, and there it remains to this day. Eventually,
the bitterness died out, and in time, the story of the Grand
Lake massacre died out too. Most Coloradans are unaware
of the bitter feud and the deaths that resulted in Grand
Lake long ago over the struggle by men for power and
control. Only their choices went to their graves with them.
Maybe those choices became inscribed on their souls, to
accompany them wherever they went in the next life.

Native Americans who called Colorado home before
the white wave rolled west knew that the lake and its surrounding landscape were special places. The Ute, Arapaho, and Cheyenne all took advantage of the beauty and
bounty of Grand Lake. At times their paths crossed. Sometimes this led to battles for horses or to control access to
hunting or rights to establish summer camps. Several famous Grand Lake legends arose from the Native American
heritage in Grand Lake. Are they true? I cannot tell you.

The same types of struggles that took place in Grand
Lake between the Native American tribes and between
groups of early white settlers continue. As always, it is a

struggle for power and control. As of this writing in 2016, it is a fight between those who wish to preserve the natural beauty and resources and landscapes of Grand Lake and those who wish to develop the land, utilize the resources (water) unencumbered, and increase tourism. Many locals wish to keep Grand Lake as it was in the "old days." My wish is for compromise that might ensure reasonable growth and protections. Durango Pete simply wishes to walk through a town that he recognizes, to have some open spaces to run free, and to have the spectacular clear waters of the lake for a swim now and then.

There are two Native American legends about Grand Lake, known as Spirit Lake by the Native American tribes. The Ute Legend of Grand Lake tells the story of a group of Utes camped at the lake who were attacked by a band of Arapaho (and possibly Cheyenne). The Ute women and children were gathered up and placed on a raft in the lake to escape the enemy warriors. The raft was overloaded, and a sudden, strong wind overturned it in the middle of the lake. All the women and children on the raft perished. Many Ute warriors were killed as well. The Ute warriors eventually won the battle, and legend has it that the Utes stayed away from Grand Lake for years following the tragedy, fearing evil spirits. Some believe that the early morning mists arising from the lake are the ghosts and spirits of the women and children who drowned. It is said that in the winter, after the lake is covered in ice, you can sometimes hear the wailing and moaning of the women and children. Durango Pete and I have seen the mists rising from the lake many times; they are eerie. To this day, the Ute Indians believe the lake to be bad medicine.

The Arapaho were responsible for naming the lake Spirit Lake. The Arapaho believe that, on one December day, it was so cold that the ice was thick enough to support a herd of buffalo. Numerous buffalo tracks were visible in the snow covering the ice. The lake was completely covered in ice except for an area in the center of the lake where the water was still exposed. Tracks of a very large buffalo led from the water onto the ice, and then back again. Many Arapaho believed the buffalo was a white buffalo, a spirit buffalo that lived beneath the lake. Thus the lake was named *Spirit Lake*.

The earliest white settler to put down roots in Grand Lake was Judge Joseph Westcott, who arrived in 1867. After being swindled out of some property, he had homesteaded near Hot Sulphur Springs, twenty miles southwest of Grand Lake. Judge Westcott found a lone Indian camped near the lake who told Westcott the tale of the Ute Indian tragedy. Westcott was so taken with the story that he penned a poem in honor of the tale.

I remember, many years back, on a summer fishing trip when I was a young boy, my dad telling me and my brothers the story about the Ute battle and the women and children who drowned. We were seven or eight years old at the time. It has stayed with me all these years. I continue to look for the Ute spirits and listen for the sounds of their voices every time I am at the cabin with Cynthia and Durango Pete—and when we walk or sit by the lake.

On this day, as Pete and I sat on the bench looking at the peaks that surround the lake, and as we looked at the beauty of the water and Shadow Mountain standing sentinel over the lake, I thought about those souls who came before Pete and me, and their struggles. I thought about our present battles in the world for power and control and ownership. I thought about points in my own life where I was engaged in, and damaged by, just such fights. Then I thought, once again, about my early struggles with Durango Pete—to win, to be in control of our relationship. I gave thanks for the release, the epiphany that allowed a relationship to grow between a man and a dog. As Pete and I sat there, I came to know the struggle immortal. I came to know the importance of history, and hard self-evaluation, and the difficult task of letting some things go. Pete and I started this poem in honor of the day's inward journey, our ramble through town, and our repose by the lake. We wrote it in honor of those who came long before us and who loved the landscape as we do. I finished the poem later that night, as Pete slumbered by the fire.

Children of the Mist
By Stephen Hinman & Durango L. Pete

The Moon of the Falling Leaves sleeps upon the
mountain's breast
And lies down upon the lake that rocks, easy with the
pull and push of moon and breeze.
In the lap of the lavender glow,
the Children of the Mist sing.
I hear their voices, small and sweet.
Native words, soulful and sad,
sail into the starry night

To slip between then and now.

In the echo of the whistling elk,
the Children of the Mist dance.
I see their shadows spin and stoop
and hear the drumbeat,
The hollow thump of bass, and the wave's gentle slap.

Under the wisp of waffled clouds and the sway of dark
pines, the Children of the Mist mourn.
Mothers with their cradleboards,
and the Old Ones crooked, walk
And they rise from ancient waters deep,
to linger for a moment.
In the creeping chill a coyote calls.
The force, timeless rolls down from the Kawuneeche
And the Children of the Mist
lay down to sleep once more.

CHAPTER 10

"The Water Finds the Right Path without Thinking."

Mr. Steve & Durango L. Pete

EARLY IN MY RELATIONSHIP WITH Durango Pete, when I struggled to know who Pete was, what he needed, and how to establish a mutual trust, understanding, and connection, I had contacted the animal communicator for help. She had given me confirmation of what I had already suspected about Pete—his wild nature, his profound intellect and need to be challenged, and his reluctance to be constrained—physically and by the conventions of life in a home in suburbia.

This awareness of who Pete was and the memory of *Kinship With All Life* were on my mind one day. It was a fine winter day, about six months after we had adopted Durango Pete. The sun was shining, and it was warm for the time of year. Pete and I needed some exercise. Previous snows and cold weather had kept us housebound too much. I decided it was a fine day to gypsy-foot.

The animal communicator had helped me understand that Pete needed opportunities to be off his leash and to go where his nose and whimsy led him. This day was to be Pete's to shape. We would go where he said we should. J. Allen Boone had discovered how to gypsy-foot, as he called it, during his developing relationship with the famous movie dog Strongheart, a very intelligent German shepherd.

One day, on a typical walk, in which Boone was the arbiter of where they would go—typically the same route leading from the guest cottage on the estate, where the producer and Strongheart's master had ensconced them in his absence—Strongheart refused to go any farther. He simply sat down on his haunches. Boone was perplexed. Then, after a short while, he received a message from Strongheart. Strongheart wanted to go another way—he wanted to lead. Boone sent an image back to Strongheart, "OK, boy, lead on. We will go where you want to go today. We will gypsy-foot."

Strongheart led Boone on a great walk into the California hills above the estate. Through Strongheart, Boone found places and landscapes he had no idea existed so close to home, and he came to understand that he was not superior to Strongheart simply because he was a human. Boone came to believe that he and Strongheart were equal partners in the journey we call life here on Earth.

I was beginning to trust my own instincts about Durango Pete. I was learning that he was communicating with me in the same way that Strongheart had communicated with Boone. The words and images that often popped into my head when I was with Durango Pete were coming from him. They were not merely figments of my imagination. Sometimes I needed to pay attention to him—to what he needed, what he wanted—and to let him express his own existence as a living, breathing being equal to me in importance and complexity. His wild side needed to be exercised too, not only his legs, lungs, and heart. So on that fine winter day, Pete would lead and I would follow.

Durango Pete led me away from our house and headed northwest on the paved trail system through our neighborhood. Pete was on his leash for this part of the trip, but I let him lead the way, and at every trail intersection he made the choice about which fork to take. Soon, he led us off of the paved trails, across a road, and onto a dirt jeep road called the Highline Canal Trail.

After we had traveled two miles, Pete turned left onto a single-track dirt path and downhill toward the flats that sit east of the South Platte River. The landscape is dotted with rabbitbrush and yucca. Rabbitbrush is one of my favorite plants. It is so named because it provides great cover for rabbits trying to avoid predators. In the winter, rabbitbrush sports brushy dry blooms on the ends of stalks. The blooms are a lovely golden color in the winter months. When the sun hits them right, they are dazzling—like thousands of golden coins. This is how they looked as Pete started through them. He stopped and sat down. I knew immediately that he wanted to be released from his leash. I reached down and unhooked the clasp holding the leash to his collar. I was not sure that I got a thank-you, but off he went, free at last. I followed fifty feet behind.

Shortly after the Chatfield trail split from the Highline Canal Trail, the path divided into three alternate routes. The eastern split stayed the highest, skirting a mesa. The middle division dropped down into a gash in the mesa that ran in a north-south direction. The western trail passed through a thick stand of willows and then into a wide, open meadow adjacent to the eastern shore of the South Platte River. I was unsure which split he would take. Pete chose the middle path—through the gash in the mesa. The middle path traveled slightly downhill to the north, through a narrow valley. Soon I discovered why Pete had chosen the middle fork. The little valley we entered was bright and sun filled. Durango Pete and I named it "the little valley that captures all the sun." The little valley offers a microclimate; it captures any sunshine present, and it holds it and the warmth within its narrow, sloping walls. I now know that it is always a nice stretch to walk during the cold-weather months. It certainly felt like summer in the valley on that day.

The path swung to the left and headed west toward the river. Suddenly the valley opened up, and there stood the ruins of an old homestead. What a surprise! Of course, Durango Pete immediately headed for the tumbledown cabin on a beeline. He sprinted through the open front door to explore the inside of the old shack. Since Durango Pete had chosen the path that day, and because he was in the lead and the first to discover the ruins, the log cabin became known to us as "Pete's Place." That was also the day that Durango Pete earned another nickname, "The Chatfield Rambler," because it was his ramble to make and he chose the landscape near Chatfield Reservoir.

The front of the cabin faced northeast. It had windows adjacent to the door and a view of a large meadow and wetlands and the giant old cottonwood trees that line the banks of the South Platte River. From the rear of the cabin, the land rose gently to the southwest, and Pete and I could see the mountains peeking over the ridge. I have done some research, trying to find out who homesteaded there and built the old cabin, but I have not been successful. The cabin remains Pete's Place for the time being, in honor of his discovery and the serendipity that comes from a cattle dog leading the way.

Often when Durango Pete and I gypsy-foot, when we simply follow our noses without too much thinking, when we let an adventure or outing simply flow like water, we find unexpected surprises—physical and existential. The log cabin was one such example.

Durango Pete and I found an old log near the cabin on which to sit. We sat on the bluff behind the cabin that overlooked the South Platte River far below. We gazed at the mountains to the west. It was a beautiful riparian setting. While we sat there enjoying the view, I suddenly remembered that I had been in this same general area long ago—when I was a little boy of eight or ten. My grandparents had owned a bar-restaurant near the very spot where Pete and I sat on the log. I told Pete the story of my Granny Martha and Grandpa Bill.

Grandpa Bill was my stepgranddad but the only grandpa on my father's side that I ever knew. My paternal grandfather by blood, Merritt Charles Hinman, died in 1935. He was stabbed in the back in a Leadville saloon. His construction company, Hinman Brothers Construction, was doing work at the Climax Mines and Fremont Pass near Leadville at the time. The family rushed him to Denver from Leadville, but he died in Denver the next day. His lung was punctured by the knife blade and had collapsed. He developed pneumonia from the mortal injury.

Granny Martha was a real Colorado woman and a pioneer lady. She was born and raised in Palisade, Colorado, on the Western Slope. She was plainspoken and tough, honest as the day is long, and a ton of fun. Grandpa Bill, my stepgranddad, was of German descent: William Ochsner was his name. He was one of the hardest-working men I have ever known. He was lean and rawboned, and he had a grip like steel. He was meticulous in his appearance, and he kept everything he owned the same way—neat as a pin. In fact, he made my Granny Martha remove her shoes before she got into the car—especially if it was his big, cream-colored Packard convertible with the red leather interior.

I reached down and gave Pete a bit of a cracker with cheese, and then I continued the story.

Granny Martha and Grandpa Bill were entrepreneurs. In the 1940s, they owned a nightclub in downtown Denver called the Club Havana. It was quite the hotspot at the time. They booked a wide variety of entertainers to perform on the main stage, singers and dancers mostly. My older brother still has the billing photos of many of the stars they booked at the club. I remember seeing a photo of Gene Kelly sitting at the bar.

Eventually, tastes and times changed, and business began to slow. My grandparents sold the nightclub. After the nightclub closed for good, Grandpa Bill started his own trucking business. At first, he drove long-haul rigs, and my dad used to work for him sharing driving duties, loading and unloading freight and handling the business accounting and managing the books. I remembered hearing stories about trips they made in the dead of winter over La Veta Pass and Wolf Creek Pass in the southern mountains of Colorado. They had some hair-raising adventures. But they were both young then and not afraid of much.

In 1962, Grandpa Bill was hauling coal up to a processing plant near Hayden, Colorado, west of Steamboat Springs. It was a weekend, and Grandpa Bill was working alone. There were no plant workers on duty that day. He dumped a load of coal into the coal hopper and fired up the conveyor belt and crushing apparatus. The machinery groaned to life and did its work. But after a bit, the gears in the hopper jammed. He could not unload the remainder of his coal with the hopper jammed. He knew that there was an access panel on the hopper where he could see the gears and determine the problem. Grandpa Bill climbed up to the top, to the access panel. He unfastened the latches and opened the access door. He could see that the large gears were jammed where they meshed by a large chunk of coal. He stepped inside with one foot and kicked at the gears to free the jam. He kicked the gears several times more, and they freed. But he slipped in the process, and the gears pulled his leg into the mechanism, crushing his leg between the teeth. The gears jammed again, with his leg now hopelessly pinned. He cried out for help and in pain.

There he remained for nearly three hours. Several hours later, a hunting party happened to pass nearby and heard Grandpa Bill's calls for help. One of the members of the elk hunting party was a doctor. He quickly assessed the situation and determined the only thing they could do was amputate the pinned leg to free Grandpa Bill. They had the saws and knives they carried to dress the elk, so they put those to good use. What kind of man can survive three hours trapped with a hopelessly crushed leg and then endure an amputation with crude instruments and no anesthesia? My Grandpa Bill.

The rough surgery proved successful, in part due to a tourniquet that was fashioned out of his leather belt and that staunched the flow of blood from the rough knife and saw cuts. After he was freed, the hunters rushed him to the hospital in Craig, Colorado. The doctors there had to perform another amputation to clean up the work done hastily at the coal plant.

Grandpa Bill survived and was interviewed by the local paper. They asked him, "How did you manage to survive such a horrific ordeal?" Grandpa Bill answered, "I kept thinking about my three stepgrandchildren. They kept me alive." That was my grandpa. And I loved him no less than if he had been my own flesh and blood. He could not have known what would happen that day when he drove his truck toward Hayden with a load of coal. Life takes us all largely where it will.

Grandpa Bill was a fighter. Once his leg was healed and he was fitted for his prosthetic leg, he started planning how to continue his trucking business. He sold his big rig and purchased two brand new Dodge dump trucks. He had them fitted with automatic transmissions and hand controls so that he would be able to drive them despite his missing leg. The trucks were painted two-tone colors of deep burgundy and cream. He kept those trucks as spotless as his Packard—not an easy thing to do with dump trucks. He had custom air-horns installed, and we boys loved to ride with him in the trucks and pull the chain to sound the big horns. If he was on a big job, with many other haulers working too, they raced one another to be first to get a load, weigh-in, drive to the work site and release their loads by tipping the hydraulic dump bed up until the load slid to the ground. It was fun to ride along—and a bit crazy too.

After a while, driving the trucks and keeping them maintained became too much for Grandpa Bill. The economic conditions at the time also played a part in Granny and Bill deciding to sell the trucks and quit the trucking business. Soon they were back in the nightclub business. They bought a bar and grill southwest of Denver near the Martin Marietta (now Lockheed Martin) plant and close to Waterton Canyon, the canyon where Durango Pete and I sat.

One might think that my grandparents planned every move and decision in their married life. There is no doubt in my mind that they discussed things and that they made informed decisions to the best of their abilities. But I also know that they were confident people and they trusted their instincts and that things would work out. They had sort of gypsy-footed their way through life.

They called their new nightclub the Bill-Mar Lounge. It became a popular after-work hangout for the employees of Martin Marietta and others who lived and worked near Waterton Canyon. Of course, my brothers and I loved every chance we got to visit Granny Martha and Grandpa Bill at the Bill-Mar Lounge. The place was kept spotless, and the food was outstanding. Granny Martha was one of the best cooks I have ever known. She cooked old-style and home-style. Everything was made from scratch and was fresh—purchased from the truck farms located on the outskirts of Denver. I loved to hang out by the jukeboxes and pinball machines. Then, when I was weary of the games and music, I was given permission to sit at the bar and have a Coke, a cheeseburger, and the best homemade french fries ever.

When my grandparents got older, long after the Bill-Mar lounge was no more, my parents sold our childhood home on Nielsen Lane, and they bought a larger home close by to move Granny Martha and Grandpa Bill in with them and care for them. Grandpa Bill began a long, slow decline. Eventually, he was too sick and weak to wear his prosthetic leg, and he no longer had the strength to get around using his crutches. When I was home from college during holidays and during the summers, I helped carry him from his recliner to his bed, and I helped get him to the bathroom. It was an honor and a privilege. Grandpa Bill passed away in 1978. He was seventy-three years old. Granny Martha lived with Mom and Dad for another seventeen years before she finally joined my Grandpa Bill. I sure miss do miss my Granny Martha and my Grandpa Bill.

When I was done telling Durango Pete the story about Granny Martha and Grandpa Bill, and the fact that the Bill-Mar Lounge now rested at the bottom of Chatfield Reservoir near where we sat on the log, Durango Pete looked up at me, cocked his head, and told me, "That's a great story, Dad. I want to swim down there, Dad—where the Bill-Mar now sits under the water—and have a cheeseburger." He sure can make me laugh!

I learned from Durango Pete a lesson that I had known

long ago, when I was a little boy. Like most of us, I had forgotten it. It's easy to do when you fill your head with stupid stuff, when you become focused on getting somewhere you think you need to be. Maybe it's that old control thing—the desire to deny chance or fate or the wishes of others to tell you what to do. I realized, as surely as my Grandpa Bill must have come to know on that fateful day hauling coal, that the idea that we are in control of the events in our lives is largely a myth. When I was little, none of these things mattered. I was like a mote of dust. I went were my fancy took me—within reason. Thanks to Durango Pete on that sunny winter day, I got to visit my grandparents and an old memory long forgotten. Often the best days, and the best adventures, happen when you simply gypsy-foot along, when you empty your head of big human things and you let your mind go like water that is free, and you simply follow where you're led by your nose and whimsy and a warm winter breeze—and a wild little cattle dog named Durango Pete. Pete and I wrote a poem about this: about how it is to be a little kid, how it is to let your mind wander like a stream, and how it is when things are simple. A dog can lead you like a river, back to places long forgotten, and to new places—inward and outward.

Once

By Stephen Hinman & Durango L. Pete

Once, I sprawled wide in the mowed grass
And I watched clouds of gauze
Slide past in a cerulean sea.

Once, I put my hands in the dirt
And I felt the gritty grains slip away.
I walked barefooted in the world
And I squished joy between my perfect toes.

Once, I put my tiny hand through the light
To see my own translucence
And I tickled motes of dust that danced in the beam.

Once, God was simple.

CHAPTER 11

"Fear Is a Powerful Provocateur."

Mr. Steve & Durango L. Pete

TIME DOES WHAT TIME HAS a habit of doing—passing. The older I get, the faster it passes. It is one of the great juxtapositions of life: as a child, when I had lots of time, I had relatively little patience with it. Now that I am much older, in my sixties, I have little time left, and I am much more tender with how I use it.

I should not have been surprised that the time with Durango Pete was accelerating too. I had been too busy juggling the changes brought by bringing a cattle dog puppy into our lives. But by that time Pete was seven months old, I was not consumed by fears and doubts and worst-case thinking, and new space had begun to open in me and in my relationship with Durango Pete. In the beginning, I had many fears about what we had done in adopting him and about how things would turn out. Would he learn to love and trust us? Would he be too wild for life in a suburban household? Would he be good with our grandchildren? Would I have the patience and energy to stick with his training and to provide him the exercise and stimulation he needed? I think these fears were largely rational. But they provided a negative form of motivation for me. And, as such, my fears hindered the development of my relationship with Durango Pete. Fear keeps us anchored in place when the soul needs room to roam and the freedom to fail.

As time went on, Pete and I made progress in all areas about which I had been so fearful. The biggest gift that time gave me was the loosening of my grip on Pete and the lessening of my fears about our future with him. In the places where fear had dominated and had been the provocateur of rough handling, beautiful things began to bloom: trust, charity, empathy, release, and joy. In short, I began to love Durango Pete. I didn't love him because he was handsome or because he did what I demanded. I loved him for who he was and for where he was leading me. I hoped that I was holding up my end of the bargain and that he was enjoying the life that we were creating together.

These thoughts rolled through my head on a late February day as the three of us—Durango Pete, Cynthia, and I—drove south from Denver in our wagon, headed for New Mexico and Arizona on our first big road trip together.

Cynthia and I thought Durango Pete was ready for a long trip and a change of scenery. As for us, we were weary of winter. My autoimmune arthritic condition, ankylosing spondylitis, had me in a flare-up. Cold weather always makes my arthritis worse. I was suffering, and I longed for warmer temperatures and sun. Cynthia and I put together a trip to Arizona. We planned to stay a month in Tucson, and Pete would be joining us. By the time we returned to Colorado, spring would be around the corner. We knew that traveling in the car was not Durango Pete's favorite thing to do, but Cynthia and I love road trips, and we thought he would enjoy a break from winter too.

I am always happy to see January in the rearview mirror. It is the coldest, dreariest, and longest month of the twelve. Curse of the first-born, I guess. Durango Pete didn't seem to mind. He continued to go about his doggy business—living in the moment and enjoying most things, as usual. Time passes—a gift and a curse—and reliably, February arrived. Near the end of the month, we loaded up the car and headed south to the desert. Cynthia and I wondered if Pete would like the desert as much as he did Colorado and the mountains.

Durango Pete was situated nicely in his dog bed in the back seat of our wagon. Blue skies unfolded before us as we headed south on I-25. The mountains rose from the plains, their summits and even the lower flanks draped in heavy snow, and they kept constant company with us. Durango Pete mostly slept. Cynthia and I enjoyed the views and chatted about Colorado history. Soon we were south of Colorado Springs and Pueblo. The Spanish Peaks came into view. The Ute Indians called the peaks *Huajatolla* (pronounced Wa-ha-toy-a), which means "two breasts" or also "breasts of the Earth."

We were driving through a part of Colorado that had seen more than its fair share of misery over the years, not far from the sites of both the Ludlow and Sand Creek Massacres. As we motored along, I thought about the evil that grows when fear and greed and contempt for others take root. Most Americans know nothing about Ludlow or Sand Creek. Many Coloradans do not either. I wondered how many lives lost it takes for history books to acknowledge a horror.

Ludlow is the story of the greed of the coal barons and their fear of workers who had long been exploited organizing and rising up with demands for safety and fair wages and a modicum of respect for the hard, dangerous work they did. Greed is a manifestation of fear—fear that we won't get our fair share or fear that someone will take that which we deem is ours. Out of the fear grow emotions that deny another's rights, intellect, talents, and even their very humanity. Contempt allows many horrors to be done. On April 20, 1914, a tent colony of twelve hundred striking coal miners and their families were attacked by Colorado Fuel & Iron guards and the Colorado National Guard. Sixty-six men, maybe more, were killed by the time the conflict ended. If you want to know more about this sad day in Colorado and American history, I recommend *Legacy of the Ludlow Massacre*, by Howard M. Gitelman.

The Ludlow historical site slid by the passenger-side windows as I drove south toward Trinidad, Colorado. My ancestors were miners—coal and more. I thought about my Grandpa Bill, who had lost his left leg in the accident at the coal processing plant near Hayden when I was a little boy. Safety equipment had been neglected by the company due to the costs of repair. Greed and contempt (or at a minimum, disregard) for workers like my grandpa were more important than his leg.

To the left, where the high prairie retreated in the distance, Fort Lyon and a small stream called Sand Creek held another obscure story of fear and greed and contempt: the Sand Creek Massacre. It was a part of my family history: two of my ancestors had ridden with Colonel John Chivington when he and his cavalry attacked a camp of Arapaho and Cheyenne on the banks of the Big Sandy Creek in southeastern Colorado.

I confess to love knowing the history of my family. Not everyone finds family history important, or for that matter, interesting. My dad instilled in me my love for stories about my ancestors and Colorado history from the time I was very young. Every road trip with Dad (almost always a fishing trip in Colorado) was filled with stories of various Hinman characters, family life in the old days, and Colorado history. I loved the tales, and I pictured the faces and places he brought to life. Many of Dad's stories culminated with a moral lesson. They helped me understand who I was, why certain places resonated with me, and perhaps in part, why I am the way I am. They certainly challenged me to introspect and to examine my life and how I might improve. I looked in the rearview mirror at Pete. There was so much about him and his own ancestors that I wanted to know. I felt bad that he had been separated from his dog family at such a tender age. Perhaps it was different for dogs than it was for us. Maybe they know all that they need to know.

Cynthia had heard me tell the Sand Creek story many times. She was about to hear the tale once again. My brothers and I must have heard it a dozen times over the years, so I was carrying on a family tradition. I looked at Pete in the back seat. He opened one eye. I told him, "Durango Pete, pay attention. I'm gonna tell you a true story about some of your Hinman ancestors. It is about a dark episode in our history, Pete." I told Pete what Dad always told us about Sand Creek, "Pete, it's a stain on our family name!" And then I started the tale.

Now, I am not going to tell you the entire story of Sand Creek. It is too long for describing in detail here. There are many books you can reference, although it is important to keep in mind who the narrators are. It has been said that the winners write the historical narratives. Margaret Coel's book *Chief Left Hand* is a good place to start if you want to learn more.

You know the general story of the white expansion westward and the genocide of the Native Americans that took place under the crush of Manifest Destiny. God and greed and fear are powerful forces. It was no different in the Colorado Territory in 1864.

Two of Porter T. Hinman's sons were at Sand Creek on that fateful day: Porter M. and Platt W. Hinman. They rode with Captain Nichols in Company D of the Colorado Militia. All of the troops were under orders from John Evans, governor of the Territory of Colorado, and his appointee, Major John A. Chivington.

I can only speculate as to why the two oldest Hinman boys decided to enlist. It must have been a tense and difficult situation for the family. After all, their father, Porter T. Hinman, was a friend of Chief Left Hand and many of the other Indians who camped and hunted near Boulder, Colorado, the site of my ancestor's homestead. Even so, I can imagine that the younger Hinman boys felt a sense of duty and obligation to the settlers along the South Platte Trail who had provided room and board and assistance for the Hinman family four years earlier, in 1860. The same families had helped nurse little Frank A. Hinman back to health when he fell out of the family wagon on their trip from Iowa to Colorado. Recently, the same families had been attacked, and some of the Hinmans' friends on the South Platte Trail had been run off by the hostile Indians. Their friends in northeastern Colorado were in harm's way.

I do not think that Porter T. approved of his sons' enlistment in the militia. He was older and wiser. He was not so quick to judge or to retaliate. I know that Porter T. left the Boulder area not long after the Sand Creek Massacre and that he spent the remaining years of his life wandering near Steamboat Springs, high in the mountains near Wyoming and his youngest son. I am not sure that Porter T. ever forgave Porter M. and Platt W. for their participation in the Sand Creek Massacre. His friend, Left Hand, was mortally wounded in the attack and died within days.

Fear and greed and contempt, like so many ugly infections, are stubborn. I would take the story of my ancestors at Sand Creek with me to my grave. Thanks to my father, though, I was going to use the personal history for lighter, more generous choices in my own life. I confess that, like Porter T., I am drawn to Native American culture and spirituality, and I remember that much mischief and tragedy are provoked by fear.

Despite my best storytelling efforts, Durango Pete had slept through most of the tale. But as we approached Trinidad, Colorado, he began to stir and look out of the rear windows. It was such a beautiful February day. The sky was my favorite sapphire blue, the blue that Coloradans love so much. The air was crisp, and even though we were well south of Denver, there were still smatterings of snow here and there, lingering in the shady gullies and at the feet of the greasewood and rabbitbrush. Durango Pete made it clear that he needed a pit stop.

He was being such a good dog on his first big road trip in the car. We pulled into a service station on the edge of town and filled up the wagon. Durango Pete took care of his business, and we humans took care of ours. We all got something to drink and had a snack. Then we loaded ourselves back into the car, settled in for another leg of the long drive. I resumed the story about the Sand Creek Massacre. I am sure that Cynthia and Durango Pete were thrilled that I was once again droning on about family and events from long ago. But a good story must be told, and I had a captive audience.

I finished the long historical tale about the time we got to Las Vegas, New Mexico. Cynthia had caught bits and pieces only, her slumber in the car being fitful, as it commonly is. Durango Pete was restless too, endlessly trying to find a position that he could tolerate for longer than thirty minutes.

Once Durango Pete had awakened, Pete and I discussed an adventure to visit the site of the Sand Creek Massacre. We agreed that the trip should take place in November, when the attack had happened. I had started a long poem about Sand Creek that wasn't finished. I thought that I needed to stand at the very spot where the horror had taken place before I could finish the poem. I thought that I needed to feel the chill of the November air and that I needed to smell the earth and see the landscape that beheld such a thing. The only way past some things is to take the path directly through. Denial can be a convenient but unfaithful bedfellow; I had unfinished business at Sand Creek. My dad had never flinched. He did not sugarcoat the involvement of our people who had been there. I wanted to kneel in the windswept soil and weep and ask for forgiveness.

As it turned out, in a flurry of unexpected creativity and inspiration in Tucson, I finished the poem. Of course, Durango Pete and I still plan to visit the sacred site of Sand Creek as I have described. But that is another story for another book.

The Song of Sand Creek

This is the place where the crying began.

The People of the Blue Sky should have crossed over
in the shadow of the mountain they called Two Guides.
The old ones should have rested in the cradle of
Valmont and drifted off to the music of Boulder Creek
and the Saint Vrain dancing gay and grand.
But lust and fear and greed and God said it was the
white man's destiny.

This is the place where the crying began.

The women should have prepared for winter in the way
Hichaba Nihancan and Grandmother Earth had provided
for a century before the white wave rolled west.
The children should have played in the wheat grass,
with the dogs dashing to and fro in the first snow of the
North Season.
But the beaver and the buffalo were a dream, and the
flood of the fertile flesh would not be denied.

This is the place where the crying began.

The warriors and the braves should have been on the hunt, free and fabulous like the eagle on the wild wing and the wolf fearsome and fat.

The lodges should have been many and magnificent in the meadow, warm in the wonder of the rolling hills and the smoke of the hearth fires curling up to the clouds.

But hate was heavy upon the land and the murderous militia was raised and ragged on an eager edge.

This is the place where the crying began.

The People were starving and sick
and the game was gone.
They wandered south to Fort Lyon on foot
and on ponies thin and weak.
Left Hand led what was left of the Arapaho.
Black Kettle led the Southern Cheyenne, mostly
women and children, and the old warriors
with teeth broken and hair thin and gray.
Chivington and the Colorado Third pushed south, the
devil ready to deal the damage dark and dangerous.

This is the place where the crying began.

It was the November of the Brittle Moon.
The coyotes' calls crept along the cold white bluffs and
sent a shiver through the smoky lodges spread along the
Big Sandy.
Black Kettle and Left Hand flew the Stars and Stripes
to signify.
They slept a weary sleep, believing they were safe doing
the white man's bidding once more.
The 100 daysers were dead tired.
But they were done with the doubts and they were full
of dark things,
"Nits make lice," said Chivington, and that was all
that was needed to know.

This is the place where the crying began.

In the smoky light, the delicate sleepy dawn was
shattered!
The earth trembled with the pounding of horses'
hooves and cannon crashing.
The charge was cruel.
The air was full of danger and death and the crack of
carbines
And the Blue Sky People bled in their lodges where
they lay
And in the creek bed where they fled—desperate.

Women and children were cut down on their knees
where they pled for mercy.

This is the place where the crying began.

Black Kettle stood before his lodge, holding the Stars
and Stripes.
He called out to his people, "Be not afraid! The sol-
diers will not harm you!"
White Antelope, palms outstretched and turned to the
heavens pleaded, "Stop! Stop!"
And then he began to sing his death song.
"Nothing lives—only the earth and mountains."
Left Hand, arms folded, would not fight his friends.
But bloodlust was unleashed and the hot lead flew to
the mark.

This is the place where the crying began.

What horror helped itself!
What terror tumbled from the ragtag troops!
Dismounted, the troops dismembered and dissected
the remains—
To be displayed in Denver
People lined the streets to hail the heroes'
homecoming.

How many lies were told?
How many promises and hearts were broken?

This is the place where the crying began.

The buffalo were but a dream.
And the sea of grass blowing free in the wind was a
tired, ancient vision.
The Blue Sky People were broken and removed to the
reservation.
Some of the young braves were wild.
They refused to farm and grovel for handouts.
Soon most of them sang their own death songs.
They were sung to the thrust of the saber and the thud
and terrible thump of lead.

The heart is not yet healed.
The price for treachery and wanton murder has not
been paid.
Land cannot be stolen
And a way of life, strangled and starved and children
slaughtered.

The wind wanders the high plains and the shadowed
foothills, looking for home.
The hawk and the eagle scream

And fly to the sun and the heavens—looking for the
justice of gods!
Far below, the cottonwoods weep white tears for what
they have seen.
And the Big Sandy scrubs the bones and the bloody
sand of this hallowed place.
But the stain remains stubborn and sick.

This is the place where the crying began.
This is the place where the crying began.

CHAPTER 12

"THE WORLD IS A CONFUSING PLACE— BUT TRUE LOVE SHINES LIGHT ON IT ALL."

MR. STEVE & DURANGO L. PETE

I OFTEN WONDERED ABOUT DURANGO Pete's parents and ancestry. Granted, we had him with us from the time he was about eight weeks old, but as my parents shaped me in some part, and as I inherited certain genetic traits from my ancestors, I was certain that part of the mystery about who Durango Pete was might be found in knowing more about his birthplace and his arrival in the world. The trip south to New Mexico presented a chance to put a few more puzzle pieces in place.

Cynthia and I did not have a great deal of information about Durango Pete's history. We did know that he had been rescued by an organization in Moriarty called Under My Wing. We knew that Under My Wing had placed Durango and his littermates with Colorado Puppy Rescue a short time later. Pete had been placed in a foster home in Denver for a week or so, and then he and his littermates had been put up for adoption. The event took place at a Petco near my childhood home, where we found him on that day that I went looking for another dog, a terrier mix.

Cynthia had the adoption paperwork with us in the car in a file labeled "Durango Pete." As we drove along in northern New Mexico, she was successful finding a phone number for Under My Wing. We decided to call it and see if it could give us any more information about Durango Pete's original owners. Cynthia dialed the number on her cell phone and was directed to voice mail. She left a message.

In a little while, Cynthia's phone rang. It was a lady named Pauline. Pauline, for all practical purposes, is Under My Wing. Cynthia told Pauline who we were, about Durango Pete, and that we were driving in New Mexico as we spoke. Pauline said that she would pull the records that she had and that she would see if she could find any additional information about Durango Pete. She also said that she would love to see Durango Pete and meet us. She gave us directions to a meeting place in Moriarty. Before long, a short distance west of Santa Fe, we left the interstate and headed for Durango Pete's place of birth.

New Mexico has a fascinating landscape. It is a place of stunning beauty and staggering desolation. It is also a place of magnificent wealth and heartbreaking poverty. It is a land of stark juxtapositions. Moriarty is located on a plain north of Albuquerque and southeast of Santa Fe. In February, there is not much that is green. On that day, pale blue skies arched from the heavens, and were greeted by the tan earth reaching out in all directions, until the mountains in the distance were met by a gradual uplift of the brown earth.

The city of Moriarty is named after the first white family to settle in the area, in 1887. Michael Moriarty and his family left Iowa looking for warmer weather. The land was suited for grazing cattle, and most of the early inhabitants were cattle ranchers. In the early 1900s, a railroad was built that passed through town. The railroad was constructed to provide connections to El Paso to the south and Chicago to the northeast. The advent of the railroad brought settlers looking for land from states in the Midwest. In 1937, Route 66 was rerouted and passed through Moriarty. By the early 1950s, tourists traveling the famed highway and the development of irrigation for the farms and ranches led to a spurt of growth in Moriarty. But the construction of two interstate highways, I-25 and I-40, and the dismantling of the railroad conspired to end the growth and played a pivotal part in Moriarty's eventual decay.

Cynthia and I saw mostly well-worn or tumbledown houses and outbuildings, a community largely in disrepair and forgotten by the march of time and migration to larger towns and cities. It was easy to imagine Durango Pete and his siblings being born into difficult circumstances in a home similar to those we watched pass by. It was easy to see how he might have been kept in a small pen with a dirt floor, along with his tired mother and hungry brothers and sisters. It would not be surprising that the owners would consider giving up yet another litter of puppies. It did not appear that many of the residents of Moriarty were wealthy.

By now, Durango Pete had gotten up from his bed in the back seat, and he was looking outside intently. His ears were straight up, and he scanned the scene passing by, looking right, then left, and finally straight ahead out of the front windscreen. He seemed to be saying, "I know this place!" I got a message from him that hinted of rising anxiety. "You aren't going to leave me here, are you, Dad?"

I kidded him a bit and said, "If you decide to be a good boy instead of a dingo-bat, then maybe we will keep you with us."

He said, "I will be very good, Dad!"

Before much time passed, we were on the outskirts of town. We arrived early, so we found a small park directly across from the place we were to meet Pauline. It was a rare grassy place where we could take Pete for a walk. He was happy to be out of the car. Up went his tail and ears, and off we went to explore the little park. Pete engaged in a great amount of stopping to sniff things, some rolling around on stuff, and eventually a bathroom break, much to our relief.

Pauline rolled up in a cloud of dust, driving a well-used SUV. She climbed out of her car, and we headed over with Durango Pete to meet her. Pauline was not an imposing figure. In fact, she was quite tiny. But she exuded a familiar western pioneer-woman sort of toughness and honesty. Her silver hair was a bit mussed and was parted slightly to one side of her head. Her skin was creased and lined from time spent outside in the harsh, dry climate of the West, and there were clear hints that her age was just to the far side of a half-century. She had a twinkle in her eye and a slight smile, which broke into a large grin when she spied Durango Pete. Of course, Durango Pete was just as excited to see Pauline. She had saved his life. It was fun to watch Pete greet Pauline. He has certain people for which he saves his special greetings. Cynthia and I had learned who they were by simply watching the quality and quantity of Pete's exuberance with them. He knows them immediately.

Several months before, the animal whisperer had told me, "Durango will tell you who you can trust and who you cannot." Durango and I have met many people on our walks and our adventures together. I always notice his body language and facial expressions. If it is a person who is a loving soul, who exudes peace and joy, Durango will lay his ears back and smile, and his whole body will wave side to side with happiness. His happy, wagging tail swishes back and forth in huge, joyous arcs. If it is a person who is mean and self-absorbed, Durango gives that person a cursory sniff and then turns and walks away with his ears and tail pointing straight up. He looks at me and says, "Come on, Dad. We have better fish to fry!" Pauline got the full-on "you are a person of special interest and value" Durango Pete greeting.

After much scratching, hugs, dog kisses, and general dog-human loving up, Pauline told us a bit more about Durango Pete and a lot about how she ended up in New Mexico and how Under My Wing began. Pauline told us that a local family had brought her a whole liter of wriggling, tiny cattle dogs, including Durango Pete. She told us that the family did not have the time or resources to deal with a new litter. More than that, she did not know. We would have liked to have learned more about Durango Pete's human family and living circumstances, but it really didn't matter. We were learning about Durango Pete in our own way and on our own terms. We snapped a few pictures of Durango Pete and me standing with Pauline. She told us that it was great to meet a family that had adopted a dog she helped rescue. She told us how nice it was to see that sometimes a puppy ended up in good circumstances—a success story. We said our goodbyes, loaded Pete back into the wagon, and headed on down the road to Albuquerque and points even farther southwest.

I thought about the circumstances that had brought us to Durango Pete, and he to us. It was a complex set of events, unfolding over years and across several states and many miles, bringing a dog that I didn't know existed, and who I hadn't gone to see, to an adoption event I almost missed and into our lives. The truth is that simple acts of love, and the need for it in our lives—given and received—were the driving forces behind the marriage of us with a cookies-and-cream-colored puppy we called Pete—Durango Pete. Love shone its illuminating light on events that appeared confusing and hard at the time they unfolded. A family struggling to get by in a small New Mexico town was presented with a litter of cattle dog puppies they couldn't afford to raise. They could have dumped the pups in the desert, taken the easy way out from under the burden. Many people do. But instead, they made the effort to find help, to find an organization to take the puppies. I am going to envision this effort to be one driven by love, or at least by the sort of things that are better about being human.

Then, of course, there is a woman, a small, middle-aged, tough woman who is filled with love. She is filled with love for creatures that are brought into this hard world by happenstance and often into circumstances difficult and heartbreaking. There were six or seven tiny, beautiful puppies who could easily have been tossed aside, forgotten, ignored, murdered, or simply "put to sleep." But because of her, because she could not sit by, because she was filled with compassion, empathy, charity, and a need to serve, the puppies were given second chances. Because she is a person of the light, a woman who serves love, a woman who makes a difference in the world, little four-legged lives are not only saved, but given a chance to flourish in homes and given a chance to give to their humans that which they received from her—a total stranger.

Finally, there was us—Cynthia and me. We rolled along in the high desert, hauling a cattle dog in the back seat (who, by the way, was enormously relieved that we hadn't left him back In Moriarty), headed south and west on a new adventure. We had no idea how this trip would un-fold. We had no idea how our relationship with Durango Pete would unfold. We knew that Pete and circumstances were starting to reveal who he was and that we loved him. Love—it was all because of the power of love, our need to give love, our need to receive love, that the adventure that was our partnership with Durango Pete was being written. Thank God for the love that illuminates the world. Thank God for Pauline. Thank God for Durango Pete.

Dog Treats

By Durango L. Pete
(Transcription by Stephen Hinman)

Dogs are great, and such a treat
We lie down at night, upon your feet.
We fetch your paper when you ask
For food, we'll do most any task.
We lick your salt and kiss your face
And clean our bowl without a trace.
We lead the way on every hike
And perform our tricks the way you like.
In return, a simple loving scratch
Will satisfy the torment of an itch.
A piece of turkey or some cheese
Will do, before our bedtime, please.
We know you have to pick up our poo
But remember all the things we do.
Our partnership, we like to think
Offsets the things we leave that stink.

CHAPTER 13

"WE ARE DRAWN TO THE PATH.
THE EYE HAS AN AFFINITY FOR A RECEDING LINE."

MR. STEVE & DURANGO L. PETE

"MYSTERIOUS ROADS AND TRAILS HOLD me in their spell. I have been attracted to these paths as far back as I can remember. I had the good fortune to pass through boyhood in the 1950s and '60s, a simpler time when there was no shortage of open space close to our small home in southeast Denver and when landowners were less fond of fences and more tolerant of little boys trespassing. I took full advantage of the times, gypsy-footing on my balloon-tired paper-route bike, or on foot, or both.

Road trips with Dad (usually we were headed somewhere in the Colorado mountains to go fishing) were frustrating for me because of all the paths we left unexplored. I was curious without fatigue and persistently inquisitive. Every side road and distant mountain teased me. My wild imagination was not satisfied with my quiet speculations and daydreaming. Eventually I had to ask, "Dad, where does that road go?" His answer was never satisfying. Either he responded with detailed information–history and topography–or he said, "I don't know, son."

Expertise, experience, and great details about the road or mountain killed my curiosity and strangled my imagination. If he said that he didn't know, my next question was always, "Can we go up there and check it out?" His response was quick and consistent, "No, Steve. We have to get to the river–the fish are waiting."

When I became an adult, I was finally able to fully express the part of my psyche and soul that was an explorer. I wasted no time. Durango Pete, now that he had learned some of the discipline necessary to live a life in suburban Denver relatively free of conflict, was expanding his own opportunities for free expression of his soul and his unique psyche. He had come a long way–literally and figuratively. I thought about this as the three of us made our way from Albuquerque to Tucson. We had decided not to travel only the interstates. We were going to take some of those inviting two-lanes and back roads. We would gypsy-foot a bit–by car.

The day had dawned gray, the color of wet slate. It was a brooding day for motoring. Sometimes those are the best days. We were quiet as we traveled south along the Rio Grande Valley between mountain ranges. The San Andres Mountains and the Sacramento Mountains rose to the east, across the valley floor and the Rio Grande River. To the west, right outside the passenger-side window, the mountains were much closer. Snow dusted the upper flanks of these mountains: the San Francisco Mountains and farther south, the Black Range. Even though the sun was shy, the day was a gift. It was beautiful and morose, and I was overwhelmed by my insignificance. I drove along, fully in my head and my heart. It had been a long time since I had been awash with such a profound case of the high lonesomes. The winter day was made for writing poetry and for listening to music played in minor keys. It was a day devoid of confusing shadows and brittle glare. The world outside our small windows stood in stark relief; every fold of the earth and each crack in the rocks was close enough to reach out and run a wrinkled, rough palm across.

The road was straight for the time being, so it was easy for Durango Pete to sleep soundly while the tires on the pavement hummed a song. I thought about Pete, and dogs. I wondered: were their lives like a collection of short stories? After all, while Pete slept, the car transported him to a completely different place. When he awakened, he found himself in a different landscape, with different weather, at a different time of day, and—aside from us—with different people. That thought struck me. The book I was writing, the one you are now reading, was in fact that way: a collection of individual adventures, separate from one another, but inextricably linked by the road that is our lives, Durango Pete's and mine. I had become Pete's vehicle for a journey somewhere. He had become a vehicle that was helping to deliver me to my own destination. Yes, Pete and I were on a great adventure. I had no idea where the two of us would eventually end up. I did know that wherever it was, and whenever we got there, it would be OK. It would be just as it was supposed to be. As we continued south, I looked forward to leaving the interstate, and I looked forward to the mystery of new landscapes on a two-lane I had never traveled.

When the road turns twisty, it isn't so easy for Durango Pete to stay calm, let alone sleep. I knew that soon he would be wide awake and not the least bit happy about the undulating, twisting road that crosses the Mimbres Mountains, the foothills of the Pinos Altos Mountains, and the Gila Wilderness. NM 152 would be less to Durango Pete's liking.

We passed a sign that said New Mexico Geronimo Trail. I was reading a book about Geronimo by Robert M. Utley. So this part of the drive was especially interesting. The mountains to the west, in the Gila Wilderness, were the birthplace and stomping grounds of Geronimo and his contemporaries.

Geronimo was a Bedonkohe Apache. He was born in 1829 and died in 1909 at Fort Sill of pneumonia after a fall from his horse. Geronimo was a tortured soul. His first wife and three children were killed by Mexicans, part of the ongoing fighting between the Apaches and the Mexicans. Following the murder of his family, Geronimo swore revenge. The rest is history.

Geronimo and the Apaches were also involved with raids against white settlers who made their way into Apache territory in New Mexico and Arizona. As forts were built to protect the expansion of whites looking for land, gold, and silver, Geronimo and the Apaches engaged in a series of battles. Treaties assigned his people to designated reservations, which they inevitably left, weary of confinement, longing to embrace the lifestyle they had always known and loved.

The Apaches were notorious for their guerilla warfare tactics and were feared by the Mexicans and white settlers.

The Apaches could run fifty miles in the most inhospitable terrain–terrain they knew intimately. They knew all the water sources, hidden trails, and hideouts. The Apaches, including Geronimo, were the last of the Indians to be brought under control by the white authorities. Geronimo's exploits brought him lasting fame.

The Apaches' language is Athabascan, like many of the plains Indians. It is believed that the Apaches' ancestors were plains Indians who had crossed the ancient land bridge from Asia to North America long ago. The Apaches were nomadic; prior to acquiring horses from the Spanish and Mexicans, they used their dogs as beasts of burden. Durango Pete stood up in the back seat and looked at me with his head cocked. "Beasts of burden?" Clearly, he had tuned into my reverie. I continued my thoughts. I saw Pete's face in the rearview mirror. He wanted to know more.

Their dogs were fitted with simple but elegant harnesses to pull travois loaded with the family's lodging and belongings. Apache dogs were described as mostly white with black spots and markings. After acquiring horses and mastering the skills of horsemanship, the Apaches made dogs more a part of the family, converting them to pets and sentries. Even though some Native American tribes used dogs for food, most Apaches refused to eat dog meat. The Lipan Apaches in Mexico did raise and maintain dogs as a food source. I decided not to tell Durango Pete about the Lipan Apaches. Fortunately, he had lain down in his bed and was fast asleep once again.

In Geronimo's biography, *Geronimo's Story of His Life*, by S.M. Barrett, Geronimo describes an encounter one of the women in his tribe had with a grizzly bear. The woman, mounted on horseback, surprised a grizzly feeding in a dense willow thicket. The startled bear attacked the woman and knocked her from her horse. The bear continued to attack the defenseless woman, who was then on the ground, but her little dog, which had been tagging along, went after the bear. The dog distracted the bear long enough for the woman to escape. She eventually recovered from her severe injuries, thanks to the bravery of her little dog. I wondered what Durango Pete would do if he encountered a bear—or a mountain lion. I wondered what he would do if I was attacked or injured while he and I were out on the trail in the backcountry. I had no idea. I thought about what the animal whisperer had told me about my relationship with Durango Pete. She had said that Pete and I were destined to be together. I was to teach him about living as a dog in a civilized world. He was to teach me who my friends and enemies were and how to use my natural skills.

After we had left the interstate and headed west on Highway 152, we began to gain elevation gradually. The terrain was mostly spotted with piñon and juniper. Homes and signs of human habitation were sparse. It was a lonely but strangely beautiful landscape. We passed very few cars. Certainly the fact that we were traveling in late February as opposed to the summer months was a factor in the light motor traffic we experienced. I was enjoying immensely the drive and the fact that there were so few people on the road. Soon the road began to undulate more, and we encountered our first switchback and s-curves. I could see a change in vegetation ahead. Cottonwood trees appeared where, before, there had only been cedars, junipers, and pines. In the distance, I spied the first few tumbledown shacks and outbuildings. Then we rolled into the small town of Hillsboro. There was something about this little town that fascinated me. Perhaps it was because this was the first town we had seen in quite some time. Maybe it was that the town seemed so isolated, stuck in the middle of such vast and empty spaces.

Durango stirred in the back seat. It was time for a bathroom break. We looked for a place where we could pull off the road and take him for a short walk. As we approached a curve in the road, we spied a tan stucco building on the right side of the road. It appeared to be an old service station. It looked like it might still be in operation, but we were not sure. I pulled the car off into the gravel drive adjacent to the building. There was a familiarity about the old place–like I had been there before. I could have been transported back in time, to the 1940s or the time when I was a little boy in 1955. I had tagged along with my Grandpa Bill to a few service stations just like this when he was driving his dump trucks. Time appeared to have stopped some years before in Hillsboro.

Durango Pete and I explored the exterior of the building and the grounds. It was soon obvious that the building was no longer being operated as a service station or store. No one was home, and the building was in a state of decline, to be sure. I peered into the dirty windows, trying to get a glimpse of what was inside. A screen door hung from one rusty hinge, and the faded chocolate-brown paint had blistered and was peeling away in many places. A sign said "Hillsboro."

Later on, I did some research and discovered that Hillsboro was founded in 1877. Like many mountain communities, Hillsboro had blossomed from the discovery of gold in the Mimbres Mountains, which had brought men looking for fortune and fame. In its prime, Hillsboro had a population of twelve hundred. It had shrunk to two hundred. Hillsboro claims to have had the last stage line still operating in America. I was sure that there were many stories to be told by the oldest residents of Hillsboro. But no one was to be seen. Not a child, not a dog, not an adult, and not even a bird was visible to Pete or me. Nor was anyone to be heard. It was as if Durango Pete and I were the only ones present in town. A chill brought goosebumps to my skin. Pete and I were spooked enough that he took a quick bathroom break, looking over his shoulder the entire time. His prominent cattle dog ears were folded down and back, a sign of anxiety and distress. I shuffled my feet, impatient to go; my primitive senses were keen and wary.

As soon as Pete was done, we hustled back to the car and Cynthia, who was waiting there. What did he sense that had him so uneasy and disturbed? Why was I so unsettled by the place? I don't know the answers. I only know that we both felt a presence there.

We climbed back into the car and drove quickly out of town, the Hillsboro sign and the old beige building fading slowly out of sight in my mirror. Later, when we were safe in Tucson, Pete and I wrote a poem about our eerie Hillsboro, New Mexico, experience.

Way Place

By Stephen Hinman & Durango L. Pete

It was the day—
A sad sky, stretched thin like a gray balloon, watched me
motor along.
And the earth, dull and dripping dust, waited for something to happen—anything.

It was the place—
A forgotten piece of twisting, broken, backwater tarmac
and road signs riddled with rusty bullet holes, metal edges
ragged and rolled.

It was the time—
February, and I was fighting the wheel in fading light and
the fading of my small life
Keeping beat with the Mexican radio station and the ka-
klack of tires smacking cracks, opened up like sores in the
old road.

I was lost.
Not literally, but rather in the daze of driving and the
dream of sagging barbed wire and flickering fence posts
dancing in the rearview mirror and black birds, fixed and
then fleeting, in pitted wet windscreen glass.

Then I saw it.
The sign said slow down, and I did.
I had out-of-state plates and wanted no trouble.

It hugged the roadside—close—with a sandy drive and short
cement pad and two old gas pumps, the kind I remembered
when I was little and rode in my grandpa's shiny blue '47
Chevy Coupe.
The rectangular building was adobe, the color of stale but-
terscotch candies.
But it had red doors, big crosshatched red barn doors—two
of them, and little windows high in the adobe and set deep
like old weary eyes.

How many faces had looked in the small dark panes
squinting and straining to see, standing on tiptoes?
How many faces had stared out, looking at the same
scaly, black cottonwoods and the same steely sky and
wondered where the road led and did it make a difference if
one was going east or west?

A faded round, red Coca-Cola sign hung from one adobe
wall, and a scarred white ice chest hugged the wall with the
red barn doors. I slowed down, hooked by the splash of
color and something familiar.
Under the small flagged brown sign placed high on an iron

pole, a screen door hung limp and slightly open, daring one to enter—or leave.
The sign said, "Hillsboro Court—Vacancy."

I pulled in, by the old pumps, and climbed out.
No breeze stirred.
No dogs barked or birds called.
No voices drifted from the blistered, tumbledown shacks that lined the crusty road.

I stood there, in the greasy gravel drive, and stared at the sign.
I and a thousand ghosts shared the moment—framed in mud walls and mesquite and memories. Forgotten fools passing through, on the way from somewhere to somewhere else.

I don't know why; I walked to the old screen door.
I opened it and knocked.
The hollow "rap, rap, rap" sounded silly in the silence.
What the hell did I expect?

I stood there for a long time, feeling stupid and small.

A breeze stirred, and the sweet, sick smell of old sweat startled me.

I stepped back, and turned away.

I hurried to my car.

I heard the crunch of the gravel with each step I took, and I felt eyes watching as I walked back.

The windowpanes, clouded like cataracts, were etched in my head

The window frames puttied and peeling—trying to shed the sadness.

I climbed into my car.

I never turned to look back.

But I saw the red Coca-Cola sign for a long time in the mirror, growing smaller and smaller, until it was just a tiny, red dot burning in the distance and my knuckles white on the wheel.

The rest of the trip to Tucson proceeded without incident, mundane or mystical. But the drive through the Mimbres Mountains and our brief stop in Hillsboro, New Mexico, stayed with me. As Durango Pete and I explored many trails and washes in the desert, as we climbed rough paths lined by cholla and saguaro high into the Santa Catalina Mountains, as Pete discovered the joy of frolicking and swimming in a cold desert stream, I thought about how all of us–my dad, Geronimo, the settlers in Hillsboro, Cynthia, and Durango Pete–are inescapably drawn by a line that stretches forth into the distance. That line is the path, our path. And none of us–man, woman, child, grizzly bear, or even a dog–knows exactly where that receding line will take us. Our eyes see something that beckons, and our souls say, "Go!"

Maybe it is true that our lives are snapshots of individual moments. Maybe we play the moments back like stills thumbed rapidly, so that we see our moments as having a continuity–so that we sense that we are moving forward. I thought, "It isn't important how the film is played. Life and landscapes are rich! The horizon still beckons."

Pete asks me, "Dad, what lies over that hill?"

I say, "Damned if I know, Pete. But let's go have a look."

CHAPTER 14

"Every Love Is Tested,
and Every Test Is to Be Loved."

Mr. Steve & Durango L. Pete

A S IT TURNED OUT, OUR Tucson adventure with Durango Pete was successful, and it was illuminating. We learned a lot more about Pete, and he learned a few things too. It had been scary for us, taking off from Colorado with a cattle dog we were still getting to know and heading to a landscape so different from the high prairie and mountains to which he had become accustomed. Sometimes one needs to take a chance if one wants to grow. We took a chance on our first big road trip with Pete, and the risk paid off. We had a great time in Tucson, and we learned that Pete was as wily a desert dog as he was a high plains drifter. In turn, Durango Pete discovered the joy and heartbreak of love, he had the opportunity to display his innate skills around horses and livestock, and most importantly, Pete discovered the joy of swimming. We learned that our cattle dog was as at home in the water as any Labrador or golden retriever.

Durango Pete was a tender, inexperienced, seven months old in Tucson when he was smitten by an Australian shepherd, a beautiful blue merle named Annie. I tried to warn him that he was too young for a vacation dalliance with a pretty gal. I had been down that road a time or two. But love will not be denied, and the heart will take one where it will, even if the destination ends with the pain of rejection and heartbreak. Lessons are to be learned, human or cattle dog.

Annie was experienced—and she was a tease. The ranchette, Paniolo Ranch, where we stayed when we arrived in Tucson was her domain, and she ruled it with the knowledge that she was beautiful and with the understanding that guests would come and go, canine and human, but she would remain. After all, her humans owned the joint, and she owned her humans, as dogs often do.

I knew what she was up to from the get-go. I left the door to our guest casita open a crack while I unloaded our gear from the car. Annie cut me off as I was hauling our bags to the guest house, and she pushed the door wide open with her nose and waltzed on in to see who the latest group of interlopers at the ranch were, what they were up to, and to let us know if she approved. She wandered from room to room, sniffing each of our bags and not giving Durango Pete or us the time of day. When she was fully satisfied that we were acceptable people and not going to ransack the joint or scam the owners, she sauntered over to Pete and met him nose-to-nose for a sniff of the intimate kind. Pete just stood there, ears and tail down. And then, out Annie went.

She came back for visits whenever fancy struck her, and Pete was as mystified by her random, surprise appearances as he was her first visit. Later, after he had proved to us that he could be trusted off his leash on the ranch, we found him visiting her on the back porch of the main ranch house—her primary domain and her preferred hangout. Before long, a sort of romance had blossomed, and Cynthia and I spotted them running after each other through the agave and cactus and boulders that dotted the ranch property.

The very next day, following their romp and their running through the property, she came to our casita to check things out. She wouldn't give Pete the time of day, despite his gentle or playful approaches. Poor Petey! He was perplexed. We didn't blame him.

So it went for the two weeks we stayed at the ranchette. Of course, in the interim a new dog had entered the story, a handsome black Lab named Cody. Now Pete was involved in a love triangle—never a good thing. One day Annie favored Pete. The next day she was partial to Cody. Some days she switched back and forth, turning her affections on and off like a light switch. At the beginning, Pete and Cody were adversaries in a battle for affection. Later, they become brothers in her rejection. Fortunately, we left for our next lodging in time, before real trouble developed and someone ended up injured.

I know that Pete was baffled by the whole Annie affair. I told Pete that it was OK: "Nothing ventured, nothing gained, buddy. There are more lovely hounds in the desert, dude. Trust me, Pete. Ya just gotta walk on, pal."

We said our goodbyes to Annie and Paniolo Ranch, and we moved to a new ranchette, Casa de Caballo, on the opposite side of Tucson. It sat astride the Santa Catalina River, at the base of the Santa Catalina Mountains. It had horses and a few cattle. Once again, we had our own small guest casita and our own patio on which to lounge in the sun. Every ramble we took allowed us to pass through the main riding arena, past the pen that housed a big white bull and a cow, and finally, to cross the river, which varied in flow depending upon recent rains or snowfall. Durango Pete loved each trip.

Every outing, we made it a point to visit the horses in their stalls near the main riding arena. Pete was gentle and calm around the horses, much to our surprise. He made no sudden moves, and he did not bark or display any signs of nervousness or agitation. The horses, in turn, remained just as calm, and they often lowered their heads over the stall doors to sniff Pete. When we got to the main arena, we stopped to visit a beautiful chestnut Arabian filly that had freedom to wander the large space. Once again, Durango Pete was good with the big horse. He knew where she was at all times—especially her hooves—and he managed to stay out from under her with a sixth sense that was fascinating to see. I wondered how he would be if I was mounted on horseback? Would he make a good trail-riding companion in Colorado? I filed that thought away for the future.

Just before the river, after we had passed through the main arena, we had to skirt the big metal-fenced pen with the bull and cow. Pete was a completely different dog around them. His ears and tail went straight up. And he growled and barked at them with his piercing cattle dog yipe. He paced back and forth outside the pen, stopping now and then, standing tall on all fours, leaning slightly forward with his chest, shoulders, and neck puffed out to make him look imposing. Pete was ready for battle. If the bull made a sudden move at Pete, Pete immediately responded to the bull's thrust with a beautifully executed sideways hop. How fun it would have been to see Pete work those two beasts, or a herd of them. But they were penned, and we had a river to visit.

The Santa Catalina River was a beautiful, medium-sized stream. The bottom alternated between fine sand and small rocks and pebbles worn perfectly smooth by the water and time. Durango Pete hadn't been around a significant body of moving water prior to this—only lakes. He hesitated to cross the first time. He stood back from the edge ten yards, in his high alert stance, sort of like a bulldog at full attention. Cynthia and I took off our shoes and waded in to try and coax Pete into joining us. He stood there and barked, as if he was saying, "What! Are you guys crazy? Get outta there!"

We couldn't coax him into the water, no matter what we did or how soothing our voices were or how encouraging we tried to be. The only thing left to do was to cross over, put our shoes on, and head on up the trail, leaving him there alone, on the far side. One thing Durango Pete hates is to be left behind. It was encouraging to think that he liked us enough that he detested being left. Up the trail we went, without Pete. A hundred yards from the river, Cynthia and I ducked into a stand of paloverde trees where we could hide and watch Pete across the river.

Up and down the riverbank he paced, yipping now and then. "Hey, you guys, where are you?" We stayed very quiet. After a bit, we saw him approach the water and dab at it with one paw. He switched and did the same streamside dance with his other paw. Next, he cautiously waded in—first one paw, then two. He stood there looking down. "Where the hell did my feet go?" he seemed to ask. Then, he looked up and across the river. Slowly, high-stepping the whole way, he crossed the water to our side. After he fully emerged, he shook his body head to tail, and then he sprinted up the trail to where we were hiding.

"Mom, Dad! Did you see that? Did you see me walk across that water?" He jumped up and down on us with his wet, sandy paws, spinning and dancing in joy—and with pride.

"Yes, Petey, we saw that. You were so brave, buddy boy!" We rubbed him up and scritched him all over, praising his bravery the whole time.

Then he stopped and looked at us with his head cocked. "Don't ever do that—leave me—again!"

The rest of our ramble went without a hitch. Pete managed to avoid all the thorny things that abound on a desert trail—cholla, barrel, and pincushion cacti, yuccas, agaves, and saguaros. And on the way back to the casita, he crossed the river without hesitation. In fact, Cynthia and I were delayed for fifteen minutes as we couldn't get enough of his new-found joy, watching Pete as he sprinted up and down the river, jumping and splashing and scooping up great snoots full of water as he went. Dog joy is always worth stopping to watch and experience.

Later that night, Cynthia, Pete, and I headed to the Oro Valley to visit some Kansas City friends who have a winter home there. As we visited on the patio, enjoying the view of the sun setting on the Catalina Mountains and sharing a glass or two of wine, we lost track of Durango Pete. Soon we heard splashing sounds coming from another part of the patio. We stood to investigate. Around the corner, there was Pete, fully immersed in the garden water fountain and pool, splashing around with the goldfish, the biggest smile on his face. "Come on in, you guys! The water is fine!"

In the end, our Tucson road trip and adventure opened many doors for us and for Durango Pete. We took a chance, and Durango Pete took several chances of his own—with love and with water. We learned that Pete possessed innate skills of which, until our desert trip, we had not known. We discovered that Pete had an ancient wisdom, one that is imprinted in his genes and that manifests as the result of hundreds of years of breeding and meaningful work, and before that, from the lives of his ancestors, the dingos who roamed the wilderness in Australia. Durango Pete was born in the desert of New Mexico, but he was being raised in Colorado, in the most benign suburban setting. Even so, he knew exactly what to do in the desert landscape. He was goat-like in climbing the ubiquitous rock outcroppings and fearless once he was on top, and he only experienced one thorn in a paw the entire four weeks we hiked in the Sonoran Desert. His behavior with the horses and livestock we encountered clearly came from some place within, for we had neither exposed him to them, nor had we trained him in such circumstances.

After we returned home, Pete went on to explore the rivers and lakes near our home, and he was accomplished at bringing the largest logs we could toss into the water back to shore. Pete swims as well as any Labrador retriever. He clearly loves the water—and swimming—and neither he nor we would have known this were it not for the Santa Catalina River in Tucson.

For us, Cynthia and me, the successful trip to Tucson allowed us to expand our list of possibilities with Durango Pete. Trips nearby, in Colorado, became routine and easy. And we began to plan bigger trips—trips out of state, even trips to California and the ocean.

One day, shortly after our return to Colorado from Tucson, I thought again about the book *Kinship with All Life*. Shortly after he took on the assignment of taking care of the famous movie dog Strongheart, Boone had several illuminating experiences with Strongheart that convinced Boone that Strongheart was not simply intelligent, but that the amazing dog had a soul no less important or evolved than his own human soul. I was coming to realize that Pete was not a simple possession or a sort of simplistic Pavlovian beast to be mastered or displayed. Durango Pete was no less important than me, and he was no less deserving of the kind of respect I expected in any relationship. Kindness only, or a sort of unevolved love, were not what Pete deserved. He deserved so much more.

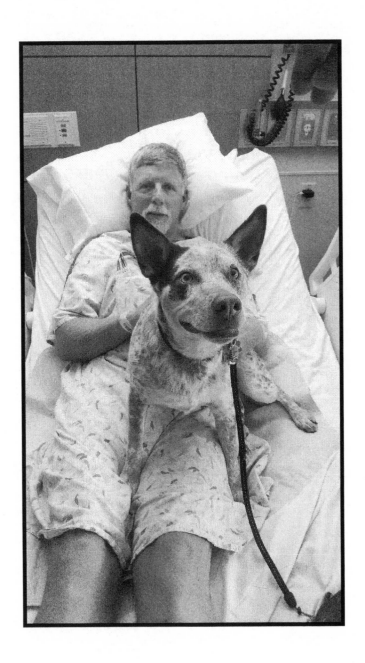

CHAPTER 15

"THE TREE DOES NOT CHANGE WHEN THE SEASONS ARE EASY."

MR. STEVE & DURANGO L. PETE

THE END OF OUR FIRST year with Durango Pete had settled into a much easier rhythm than it had during most of the first year of our partnership. Spring had come and gone quickly, as it always does in Colorado. Summer arrived with its warm days and cool nights. The heat kept Pete and me closer to home or on rambles in the higher country where temperatures allowed us to hike longer distances. Pete was now a full-grown cattle dog, and we had routines that were important for him and for Cynthia and me.

Most days were predictable. Meals happened at certain times, as did walks and playtime, end-of-the day tasks, and bedtime. I continued to talk to Pete; it was a running dialogue that surely became background noise for Cynthia. I was convinced that Pete enjoyed my consistent chatter because he talked back, using his ability to project images that arrived in my head or even sentences that popped into my consciousness, and I learned to trust that Pete was communicating back. I will tell you this: Pete can turn a phrase! And he is a damned funny dog—witty—and wit is a sure sign of intelligence. Many of the musings that title each of the chapters in this book came from Durango Pete on our rambles in nature. Pete makes me smile and laugh every day.

As the three of us moved along in a sort of benign bliss, life decided to reach out and give us a good smack upside the head, as it so often does. My autoimmune disease, ankylosing spondylitis, decided to rear up and complicate things. I was suffering a major flare-up.

Eight years back, I had undergone bilateral hip replacements, but my knees and shoulders began giving me fits. The unrelenting pain was making walks and longer rambles and adventures with Durango Pete difficult. Sleep was anything but sound or refreshing. Cynthia took up the slack that my disability was causing. She walked Pete more and more, and it was hard to stay behind. I missed our threesome and being with them in the great outdoors. I did what I could. For his part, Durango Pete adapted to the change with grace. It was nice to see an even stronger bond developing between Pete and Cynthia. That was comforting to me, and it might be very important down the road, I thought.

Cynthia played a big part in the success story that was becoming our relationship with Pete. Early on, when Pete was only three months old or less, the vet had discovered a problem with Pete's bite. His incisors were not growing in properly, in a fashion that allowed them to mesh and his jaw to close the way it should. The vet gave us a few ideas (therapies) to do at home. One of them was to play with Pete using a tennis ball. When he had it in his mouth, we were to use the ball as leverage or traction on his incisors. The object was to try and pull the ball out of Pete's mouth to stimulate his incisors to move. Cynthia became the master therapist. She did this activity every evening without fail for weeks. Pete owes his beautiful smile and proper chewing to his mom.

Cynthia and I have a sort of good cop, bad cop method of parenting although I am a soft touch mostly, not much of a bad cop. But Cynthia is more consistent than I am in disposition, and Durango Pete knows that. Mom is always good respite and comfort. Dad can be grumpy now and then. I was in a lot of discomfort, and I was more withdrawn and testy than usual, so Pete needed his mom more than was typical.

Part of my health struggles dated back to a serious mountain bike accident I had suffered in the summer of 2011. I was training for a big endurance race in Laramie, Wyoming. I was on one of my final training rides, on the Kaw River Trails near Lawrence, Kansas, riding a new mountain bike, and it was handling in a very evil way. I had fallen once and escaped with a few scrapes. I had decided to call it quits for the day, and I had told Cynthia and the gang I was riding with that I was going to hook up with the levy road and take it back to the parking lot three miles away.

Before I could reach the road, I had to ride another half mile of trail. I knew the trail well. The part coming up wasn't technical. There was a steep, smooth downhill followed by an uphill to the road. I reached the downhill and let the bike coast, freewheeling down at about twenty-five miles per hour. When I hit the bottom, I saw that a deep section of sand had washed in from the recent flooding of the river, and my front wheel washed out when I hit the sand. In a second I was slammed to the ground at high speed. I landed on my left side, with my arm between the ground and my ribs. I hear a loud *crack,* and I grunted as the air was forced out of my lungs. The pain was immediate, and I knew that I was badly injured. I lay there for several minutes, letting reality seep back in. Then I started taking stock of my injuries. I thought a broken collarbone was most likely. I reached up with my right hand, and I felt the length of the bone. I didn't feel any disruptions. Next, I decided to check for a dislocated or broken left shoulder. Even though I was on my left side, I could move my upper arm enough to see that there were no grinding or mechanical issues with my shoulder. It was then that I realized I was having a hard time breathing. I knew immediately that I had fractured a rib, or ribs, and that one of them had punctured a lung. I lay there, yelling for help, until Cynthia and the others finally arrived.

I am a physical therapist, and my medical knowledge and experience dealing with difficult injuries helped me stay calm. I told Cynthia that I was badly hurt and to call 911. There was nothing else to be done until the EMT personnel could reach me. I knew that would take some time. We were three miles in and could only be reached by an ATV. I went to my Zen place and simply focused on my breathing.

It took the medical personnel an hour and a half to get me out by ATV, into the ambulance, and finally, to the Lawrence hospital. They couldn't give me any pain medications since they did not know the extent of my injuries. It was a rough ride down the levy road, and every bump during the ambulance ride sent an exquisite jolt of pain through my chest. Again, I worked to stay in my altered state of detachment.

The CT scan revealed seventeen rib fractures, so many that the condition is called flail chest. This means that the rib cage can no longer function as the breathing assistant that it is. The scan also revealed a punctured left lung and internal bleeding. Finally, to add insult to injury, it was discovered that I was in urinary retention and that my bladder was so full that it was a miracle it had not ruptured. I had been having urinary difficulties for some time and had been working with my family physician to try and discover the root cause. I then knew that it was an enlarged prostate that was blocking the flow of urine.

The ER doctor relayed all the injuries to me and to Cynthia, who was by my side. He told me he needed to insert a chest tube to inflate my collapsed lung and to drain the blood and fluid accumulation in my chest cavity. He was a gruff old cuss—matter-of-fact with few bedside manners. He said that he could numb me up for the chest tube insertion but that the injection would delay things and that it would hurt too. He decided to go ahead and push through the chest wall without any numbing agents. I survived, but he will not be attending any of my family gatherings.

The eleven days that I spent in the hospital were a fog of pain and drugs and frightening hallucinations about Satan and his agents, a side effect of the synthetic morphine I was being given for pain. Meds were adjusted, time passed, and I returned home to our house in Kansas City.

Recovery from my injuries took six months. As I progressed, we followed up with a urologist about my urinary problems. Surgery was going to be needed to remove most of my prostate—to remove pressure that was closing my urethra and to allow my bladder to empty. Trouble does come in bunches. We had only recently lost our dog of eighteen years, Pumpkin, to old age. We had also lost our cat, Rocky, shortly after Pumpkin died. Rocky was also eighteen years old when he passed. However, it was a blessing that we were without pets during my injury, subsequent prostate surgeries, and our move from Kansas City to Denver.

Although it had been two years since my bike accident and prostate surgery, I was not only having autoimmune arthritic problems but my bladder problems were also continuing. I had to self-catheterize four times per day. My bladder had been damaged permanently by the urinary retention. Additional surgery was looming. I was torn between needing to spend more time resting and missing my rambles and adventures with Durango Pete.

At the nadir of my disability, I spent time in the hospital for several surgeries and emergencies. In my down time, I thought about my early days with Durango Pete—how frustrated I was at his wild behaviors, how I feared that I would not be up to the task of providing him the exercise that he needed, and how I wondered if Pete and I would ever connect. At that point, I was unable to walk him or take him on new adventures. I wondered if our relationship would fall apart. I missed hiking with Cynthia and Durango Pete terribly. It was great to have him around, to brighten my days with his goofy antics and his big Pete smile.

Cynthia was doing a great job carrying on in my absence.

Our kids and their wives visited me, and it helped so much to have them on my side as I worked my way through the tough times. Then, one night when I was alone in the hospital for yet another procedure and feeling down and missing Pete, the door to my room opened and in came Cynthia—and Durango Pete. It turned out that the hospital was pet friendly, and it allowed dogs to visit their owners and patients provided the visiting dog was current on vaccinations. I was overjoyed! Pete wasn't so sure at first. He is not a fan of going to the vet, and the hospital had the same sterile tiles, bright lights, and familiar smells of bleach and medicine. He sniffed everything in the room really well, his ears back and tail down, slinking from place to place. When he was done, I called to him, "Petey! Come see me, buddy boy!"

Up he came, no small task since hospital beds are tall and the floor is slick. He rubbed me up all over, and he gave me a bunch of good kisses and licks, his tongue stopping from time to time, stuck on the back of my hand to take in each of my flavors and to make sure that I was, in fact, his dad and alive. That visit helped get me over the hump. I like to say, "A person can lick most any difficulty if one lets a dog lick 'em." Durango Pete is a world-class licker. It also helps to have a great partner—Cynthia—and loving kids and grandkids and good friends. I am lucky, and thankful, to have all of them.

Shortly after we celebrated Durango Pete's first birthday in early August, I got back to my rambles with Durango Pete and Cynthia, and life settled into a routine similar to what we could call normal. However, every hardship changes you. I still have my arthritis, and it continues to get worse. I still cannot urinate on my own, and I continue to self-catheterize. I have survived a bout with bladder cancer recently. I guess we get to choose how we are going to react to the challenges that life presents each of us and what changes that hardships are going to bring about in who we are. I try to use the hardships that life has presented me as catalysts for something good. I was lucky to enter the world a happy boy and an optimist. My mom was a good example of moving forward with a hopeful, loving heart, despite the blows she received along the way. I paid attention. I'm a better man for the mistakes I have made and the pain I have experienced over the years. I am a better man because of Durango Pete. He is a gift. And I am grateful that I didn't give up on a crazy little cattle dog who demanded much and who deserved most of it.

Life is richer because Pete and I and Cynthia worked hard to turn a struggle into a partnership. I know that at the age of sixty-six, the road ahead is going to get rougher. That's OK. I am still looking forward to the adventures that await us, working through the problems that arise, and seeing what kind of man I will be and what kind of dog Pete becomes. I like to say, "And so with hardship, I shed another skin, and patiently I grow my new self, and I wait to see what kind of new art I shall be."

Pete likes to say, "Me too, Dad!"

CHAPTER 16

"SOMETIMES I HURRY BECAUSE I DON'T WANT TO FEEL RUSHED."

MR. STEVE & DURANGO L. PETE

IT'S EASY TO BE LAZY in the winter. Even the light sleeps more often during the winters in Colorado, and the cold can easily strangle enthusiasm. Heavy snows make an old man want to curl up under the covers and listen to the silence and ponder things great and small—or just sleep. But a young cattle dog has other ideas. Especially when the temperatures drop and the white stuff falls from the sky.

We discovered early on that Durango Pete did not care for hot weather. That seemed absurd, given that cattle dogs were bred for the heat and harsh conditions in Australia. Cynthia and I are friends with many other cattle dog owners, and our own daughter, Krista, eventually got a cattle dog, Blueford. Without exception, the owners all report the same trait in their dogs. In the summer, the dogs prefer to lounge about in the shade, and walks become shorter and less frequent. Pete was no exception—unless there was a job to do. A FedEx or UPS truck driving by the backyard was an opportunity to herd and too tempting to resist, heat or not. A short spurt of sprints up and down the fence line continued until the truck had been effectively chased away. This was followed by an immediate return to the shade of the ash trees and Pete's collapse into the long grass for another siesta, until another job or truck presented itself. This is how it went with Durango Pete through the dog days of summer. Often, our invitations to go for a walk were turned down with a condescending look, a pivot, and a slow walk back to his preferred place of repose. "Dad, are you kidding? It's too hot for grasshoppers out there!" (Pete typically refers to grasshoppers as "those annoying clacking things.")

Winter presented us with an entirely different dog. Pete comes to life in the cold weather months. He loved the snow from the first time he saw it and touched it, rolled in it, and scooped up great muzzles full of the cold, brilliant stuff. Only when the conditions are the most extreme does Pete display a desire to make time outside brief, or to forego an adventure, backyard or otherwise.

Shortly after we adopted Durango Pete, Cynthia and I decided to have a genetic test done to see what other dog breeds might be present in his ancestry. The test came back after a few weeks. It listed cattle dog as the predominate lineage, but the next most dominant breed in his ancestry was Saint Bernard. We had a big laugh about that result at the time. We figured a hundred and fifty dollars had been worth a good laugh. But the more time we spent with Pete in the snow, the more we wondered if the test might have been accurate indeed.

Pete's favorite winter ramble is on a trail called Doe Creek. It is located near our old family cabin in Grand Lake. The trail is not well-known, and that allows us a chance to be in winter solitude with Pete. We make our outing as long as we wish, as there are many linking trails and options for length and difficulty. Cynthia and I are typically on snowshoes or touring skis. Pete goes just as he is. He lets us handle his paws fine unless we try to put snow booties on them. It is not worth the risk to life and limb! We have used topical dressings instead, but he licks the products off. So Pete travels in the snow au naturel.

The second or third time that we did Doe Creek, in the winter of Pete's first year, we made a great discovery. Off the main winter trail, we found the remains of an old trapper's log cabin. On that day, no cars were in the trailhead parking lot. It was only the three of us and whatever wildlife we would be fortunate to see. It was a day mixed in weather and mixed in moods. We went from warm to cold, and from chattering away to silent and reflective, as the sun dashed from cloud to cloud and the light changed from bright to somber. Our jackets were zipped and unzipped as the sun and the terrain demanded. A breeze blew now and then, raising small whirlwinds of white from the surface of the snow and powdering us with cold sugar as wisps of snow blew from treetops and branches. A shy chickadee or jay serenaded us when the fancy to sing struck them. We smiled to hear their songs. Pete stopped and looked for their hideouts. Nothing larger than birds did we see on the ski in.

Durango Pete was off his leash, so he covered a much greater distance than we did. He makes it a habit to rush up the trail—far ahead of us but not out of sight—and then he stops to linger in the forest at his leisure. This day was no different. Pete rushed ahead of us so that he would not be hurried by us and he might complete his sniffing and exploring to his satisfaction. After he finished, he walked back down the trail to meet us as we skied up the incline. When his up and back trips and forays into the forest and then back to check on us were factored in, I estimated that Pete did about a third again our total distance for the trip.

After we had skied through a dense forest of lodgepole pines for forty minutes, we moved out of the heavy timber into the clearing of a large meadow where several trails converged. My mood always lightens when I escape the darkness and shadows of the forest and enter open country. We paid close attention when we were in the heavy timber. The pine beetle devastation is so great that the risk of falling dead timber is real, especially if there is any significant wind. When we reached the meadow, we put aside those concerns.

I love it when the view opens and I can see the high peaks of the Front Range, snow-covered and far off in the distance. The willows that lined the pathway of Doe Creek were in their winter splendor, their branches now orange and plum and the color of an old woman's rouge. Durango Pete sprinted ahead, as eager to be free of the trees as us, and eager to play in the untracked snow of the meadow. At the edges of the clearing, the aspens began to appear. Their tall, white and pale-green trunks reflected the light, and even when the sun was behind the clouds, the trees brightened the day and lifted our spirits.

Pete was far ahead, bounding through the deep meadow snow, burying his head underneath and tossing great plumes of powder into the air. He ran through the snow like the wild thing that he is. He ate the snow as he went, biting at it as if it was quite solid. When he found something especially intriguing under the snow, he jumped up into the air and then pounced on the snow, driving his sharp nose down into the depths of the white fluff until his entire head disappeared. There it remained until he was sure that the rodent or whatever he thought was under the snow had escaped. I have seen the foxes and coyotes do the same thing in meadows like this. Pete just needed more practice.

Around and around Pete went in the big meadow, making great dog pathways this way and that until the untracked snow was a crisscross pattern of Durango Pete's trails. It would have been fun to look down on his artwork from high above the meadow. Cynthia and I followed along on our skis. We were gypsy-footing in the snow, and Durango Pete was free to go where he wished and to take us with him.

After we had traveled several hundred yards, Pete headed for the forest at the edge of the meadow. We followed. Soon we saw what had gotten his attention. In front of us, twenty yards from the meadow's edge, sat a tumbledown log structure. Cynthia and I followed Pete to take a closer look at the ruins.

It was clear to me that these were the ruins of an old trapper's cabin. They sat at the north edge of the meadow. Durango Pete circled the old cabin, taking his time to sniff everything along his way. We peered over the walls to look inside. The roof was mostly gone. At the edge of the meadow, where the cabin sat, the snow thinned to a few inches in the sunny spots. We took our skis off and walked around the old one-room cabin, inspecting it all.

I could imagine the site in the warm months, when the brilliant white snow would be replaced by the tall green carpet of the meadow grasses in summer and the willows on the far side would be dusty green under the summer sun. I found a good log to use as a seat and dropped my pack. Cynthia did the same. Durango Pete took his own seat, in the snow by our feet. The sun had decided to grace our pause for a snack in the snow. We enjoyed our little feast of crackers and cheese. Pete was not shy about asking for more. Each bump of our legs with his nose meant, "More, please!" (The please part may have been missing.) The warmth of the sun, which was now out in full glory, gave me time to peruse the scene and to imagine the man who had looked upon the same meadow so many years before.

I would have picked this exact spot for the cabin. The cabin had the forest for protection and a windbreak. The winter winds prevail from the north and northwest, the same side as the back of the cabin and where the forest thickened. The front of the cabin looked to the south. It was greeted by the open expanse of the meadow and the willows and aspens on the far side, and the southern exposure would have helped the sun warm the cabin. There was a year-round source of water in Doe Creek, which cut a diagonal path across the meadow. The water would have attracted game and wildlife. It was a good spot for a wilderness home.

I sat there in the sun, listening to the wind gently winding its way through the forest. I wondered about the man who had built this place and lived here so long ago.

Durango Pete sat there too. His yellow eyes sparkled in the sunlight, and his nose was wet with the moisture from the snow and the condensation of his breathing. In and out through his warm, brown nostrils the air went. He was happy. And I was happy that Durango Pete was part of our family. He looked at me as I thought about how our lives had changed since he had arrived.

"I could live here, Dad," he told me.

"I could too, Pete," I said. Then, I shared some more of my crackers and cheese with him. A poem came into my head:

The Log Cabin
By Stephen Hinman & Durango L. Pete

So, you stumbled upon my tumbledown log surprise!
Was it an accident or providence?
Stay awhile and sit in silence.
The stillness always spoke to me.
Maybe you will hear the voices too.

After our snack was finished, we reclined a good while in silent reflection. I thought about the old trapper and about my own ancestors who had traveled this area frequently, as far back as 1865. I pictured the landscape and the men. I suspected that hurrying was not ingrained in these men, so unlike the constant rush in which we engage. Pete only hurries when he knows that we will deny him the time that he needs to fully be a dog. Back in 1865, there were few easy trails, and roads were rough. Men up here traveled on foot or on horseback. There was no getting from Denver to Grand Lake in a few hours. I remembered a story about my great-grandfather, Otto Hinman, and my grandfather, Merritt Charles Hinman.

In 1921, before my grandfather got married and became a father, Merritt and his two brothers, Mike and Fred, lived on the Hinman Ranch at the foot of Gore Pass, seventy miles west of where I then sat. The ranch was a large cattle ranch that had been homesteaded years before by my great-grandfather Otto and his brothers. By 1921, most of the Grand County cattle ranchers no longer drove their cattle to market in Denver. They used the railroad for transport. This saved work and wear and tear on the men and the cattle. But the ranchers were subject to pricing changes set by the railroad owners and executives, and there was no competition. Railroad charges had gone up to unfair levels in the eyes of my great-grandfather and his fellow ranchers in Grand County. The ranchers haggled with the railroad owners about the prices. But their negotiations brought the ranchers no relief. Otto, his oldest son Merritt, and a handful of other ranchers decided to forego the railroads and take the cattle to market themselves. Many experts doubted this could be done, and they predicted that many head of cattle would not survive the cattle drive and that those that did make it to Denver would lose too much weight and would not sell or would bring only pennies on the dollar.

Otto, his brothers Wallace and Mark Merritt Hinman, my grandfather Merritt Charles, and other cattlemen or entities like the Jones Cattle Co., W.L. Henry, and William Yust planned the cattle drive. The price-gouging railroad men could be damned! The men were each allowed two saddle horses and one packhorse. No wagons would accompany them. They planned to travel from their ranches, through Middle Park, and over the Front Range near where I was sitting with Cynthia and Durango Pete. The men could not dally on the trip, but neither could they hurry the drive, or the cattle would suffer too much weight loss or—worse—they could die.

In the end, the men completed the drive, the last large-scale cattle drive to market that would take place in Colorado. They traveled with the large herd from their ranches near Kremmling, through Middle Park, and over the high passes above timberline. Once over the Front Range, they continued to Denver, losing only one head from the herd. Two hundred and twenty-five steers and heifers made the trip successfully, traveling 120 miles in nine days. The ranchers' cost for the cattle drive was two hundred dollars. The railroad was going to charge the ranchers well over one thousand dollars if they had shipped via the rails. Eventually, the railroads and the increasing use of barbed wire fences by landowners ended the cattle drives for good. But it was fun to remember that a group of tough men had stood up to greed. And it was fun to think that these men who weren't in a rush, and who had courage, made a trip that few believed they were smart enough or patient enough to make.

I knew my grandfather and great-grandfather had working dogs on the ranch. I wondered if they had taken the dogs with them on the cattle drive. I wondered whether Durango Pete would be a good ranch hand and whether he would have helped herd the cattle as well as he herded the UPS and FedEx trucks. I said, "What do you think, Pete?" He said, "Enough sitting, Dad. Let's explore the rest of the meadow." So much for patience. We put our skis back on and slung our packs over our shoulders and onto our backs. We said goodbye to the old cabin, and the three of us headed back into the large, snowy meadow.

We enjoyed the warm sun and the big view. At the far side, the trail kicked up steeply, and I wanted to climb to the top. It was only three-quarters of a mile to the summit. I put my head down and started up. My goal was to complete the climb without stopping to rest. Sometimes I get silly ideas and turn a simple ramble into a competition. I forget I am not a young man any longer. Durango Pete was already well ahead of me, and I was huffing and puffing big time. Cynthia was right behind me. Pete had the advantage of youth and four-wheel drive. In a few of the steepest spots, I resorted to rest-stepping to avoid having to stop. Before long, I reached the summit. Durango Pete was already there (so as not to be rushed), looking for me.

"Jeesh, Dad! What took you so long?" He likes to tweak me.

He had the "I want a treat, please" look on his face. I gave him a couple of small dog biscuits. We enjoyed the view for a bit, and then the three of us headed back down the trail to the meadow. Pete does like to rush downhill. I think he may have been a race car driver, or bobsled driver, in a previous life. Or he simply likes the joy of a mad dash downhill, spraying snow left and right as he blazes through the turns. He always comes back up the trail with a big grin on his face. And then he turns around and does it again.

We reached the meadow quickly, but then we took our time crossing. Pete was ahead of us. He stopped and sat down. He was looking off to his right. Cynthia, behind me, hollered, "Steve, look at that!"

I wasn't sure what she meant. She was pointing past where Pete was looking. Then I saw it. It was a weasel, standing in the snow on his hind legs, looking at Durango Pete. It was a staredown—not in a tense sort of way. It was a meeting of two four-legged souls out in the wilderness. Pete made no attempt to chase or attack the weasel. The weasel stared back. Cynthia and I watched the whole thing in amazement and awe. The weasel was as white as the snow. After several minutes, the weasel seemed satisfied with things, and he disappeared back under the snow. Pete wandered over to where the weasel had been. He didn't pounce like a fox into the spot in the snow where the weasel had appeared. Pete simply sniffed around a bit and then sauntered back to us. "That was amazing, Dad," Pete said.

I replied, "It sure was, Pete. Good things come to those who take their time."

Back through the trees we went, careful to keep an eye out for precarious, dead lodgepole pines. We gave thanks for a safe trip. We gave thanks for legs and lungs that allowed us to ski in the wilderness. We gave thanks for the beautiful places where we could connect with our source. We gave thanks to our ancestors and those who had traveled the path before us. We gave thanks for diversity, for birds and weasels, and for dogs who teach us when to speed up and how to slow down. We skied in silence back to our car. And then we loaded up our equipment and Durango Pete for the drive up the road to our cozy cabin in Grand Lake. It was a good day to be a dog. It was a good day to be a dog's mom and dad.

CHAPTER 17

"A Dog and a Road Trip Can Teach You a Lot about Joy—and Naps."

Mr. Steve & Durango L. Pete

IN A BLINK OF AN eye, three and a half years passed ADP—After Durango Pete. Durango Pete was piling up new experiences and adventures at an admirable clip. In between, we still had the typical, mundane tasks of life to which we had to attend. Pete was now a full-fledged member of our family. He took the bad with the good and the rote with the new and exciting. We were discovering that Pete was as accomplished at downtime as he was at mountain climbing, swimming, or snow rambles. It was during one such period of downtime—an afternoon nap one fall day—that Cynthia and I discussed our next big road trip. Even though Pete would be going along, and despite the fact we were talking about a water trip, he slept through the entire conversation. A dog can teach you a lot about joy—and naps.

Pete had proven to be such a good swimmer, and he loved the water so much, that we decided a road trip out west to California and the ocean might be a great adventure with him. The car trip would be difficult, given his dislike of long trips by car and the fact that we would have to cross many mountain passes along the way. Durango Pete never has liked curvy roads, and the rise in elevation on the passes hurts his ears. But after our Tucson trip, we figured that we and Pete could get the job done. Our enthusiasm for introducing Durango Pete to ocean swimming and the beach was enough to diminish any of the downsides of travel. Cynthia and I were overdue for a bit of beach time as well.

Cynthia and I had both spent a good deal of time on the West Coast. We had taken many trips there during our marriage, and I had lived in Southern California for a while in the '70s. Our familiarity with California made planning the trip easy. I figured that we could make it out in two days driving. The first day would be the long day, as we had to get to St. George, Utah—630 miles away. The first 250 miles were mountain travel, and slower. I estimated that it would take us ten to eleven hours, depending upon how often we had to stop. The second day, from St. George to Laguna Beach, California, would be easy in comparison. It was only 395 miles, with little mountain travel, and would only take us seven hours to drive.

We rented a charming small apartment through VRBO (Vacation Rentals by Owner) for a month. We planned to stay in Laguna Beach from late January to the end of February. In the photos online, the apartment looked perfect. The apartment had a small living room with a wicker easy chair and a daybed, and it had a nice bedroom that was adjacent to the living room. A small, tasteful bathroom adjoined the bedroom and the living room. Finally, there was a small kitchen, painted in butter yellow and with a farmhouse sink. The kitchen had everything that we needed to dine in. The best thing about the apartment was that it was located only a block from Heisler Park and the beaches below. The main beach and downtown Laguna were a half-mile down the hill to the south.

The drive out west went mostly without a hitch. Pete hung out on his bed in the back seat of our VW wagon and gave us only a moderate amount of grief about the indignity of his confines, the quality of the roads, and my driving. Durango Pete loves motel rooms, so our stay in St. George, Utah, was pleasant. Pete commented that the accommodations at the Holiday Inn Express exceeded his expectations and that we should use those hotels often.

The second day, we stopped frequently in the Virgin River Gorge to take pictures. The day was dramatic, with low-hanging clouds draping the canyon peaks in uneven curtains of gray. Higher up the canyon walls, snow peeked out from under the mists, reminding us that, although we were dropping into the desert, winter still was the authority. The Virgin River Gorge is one of my favorite drives in the United States.

We continued west under overcast skies and reached Las Vegas in time for an early lunch. We ate fast food and then found a park where we took Pete for a nice walk in the grass. He appreciated the break from the back seat, and he took his time finishing his business. He was reluctant to leave the clearing skies, the sun, and the green grass to return to the car. I told him, "Pete, the ocean awaits! Time to go swimming!" That got him going. Into the back seat he jumped, and off we went, three happy travelers headed west for a bit of winter surf and sun. "Cowabunga!"

We stopped for a refill of the gas tank at Whiskey Pete's in Primm, Nevada, near the California state line. How could we not? Pete wanted to ride the roller coaster called Desperado near the service station where we filled up with gas. At one time, Desperado was the highest and fastest roller coaster in the world. But like my dad said to me when I was a boy, "No time, Pete! The ocean is waiting!"

The first time I had passed through Primm was in 1970. It was called State Line back then, and it was nothing like the casino operation it became.

Long ago, around 1920, a fellow by the name of Pete MacIntyre owned a gas station there. His gas station struggled to make ends meet, and it was during Prohibition, so Pete took up bootlegging. That is how he became known as Whiskey Pete. Whiskey Pete died in 1933. The story is that he wanted to be buried standing up, with a bottle of bootleg in his hand so he could keep watch over things. Years later, his body was accidently uncovered during bridge construction. Pete was moved and is now reported to be buried in one of the caves he excavated for producing his moonshine. Our own Pete had once again been lulled into a stupor by the drone of my voice while telling Cynthia the story. Durango Pete was fast asleep in his car bed.

On we went through the Mojave. Shadows and sunlight alternated on the rocky peaks the color of eggplant. The landscape was a patchwork quilt of light and dark. Every direction held mystery, and I was a little boy again, wondering what great discoveries were to be had north or south. All I had to do was leave the interstate. Pete awakened and brought me back to the present, and to his presence, as he stood on the center console between Cynthia and me. "Hey, Dad, where are we?" he asked.

I told Pete that we were in the Mojave Desert. I told him that I called it the "Morejabby" because, like the Tucson desert, it housed many spiney, sharp things that could jab you. Pete groaned, unimpressed with my play on words. He wanted some cheese from the cooler. I reached back and grabbed the package by feel. He got his snack. Cynthia dozed. His stomach adequately quieted, Pete returned to his bed in the back seat and curled up for another nap. I settled in once again, with the cruise control on and our snow tires humming along on the road. My mind drifted back to the first time I came through the Mojave, in 1970 with my high school friend Dave.

Dave and I grew up in the heyday of the surf music era—the early to mid-1960s. We were landlocked in Denver, Colorado, to be sure. That didn't stop me or any of my junior high school and high school buddies from joining in the surf scene craze. We bleached our hair blond. We wore white jeans, madras shirts, and blue canvas tennis shoes without socks. We listened to the latest Beach Boys, Ventures, and Jan and Dean songs in our rooms and in the private record booths at Lou's Music Box. We danced slowly with our girlfriends to "In My Room" and "Surfer Girl" at dances put on in the basement of the Schlessman YMCA. Some of us even formed our own surf bands. Mine was called The Outer Limits, and we played surf music through Fender Jazzmaster guitars and Fender Bandmaster amps at school and church dances. All of us dreamed of living in Southern California, or at least visiting there, to see the real thing and maybe even try our hand at surfing Huntington Beach.

High school graduation came and went in May of 1969. I still had never been to Southern California. Finally, in the summer of 1970, I had my chance to head west—even though the surf craze had passed with the arrival of the Beatles from Liverpool (I will never forgive those blokes!).

Dave and I planned a monthlong trip. He had an old but trusty 1959 Chevy Impala with a three-on-the-tree. It was painted an oxidized gunmetal gray—not pretty, but it was available, and it was reliable. We called the Impala The Gray Goose. Dave and I were both racing dirt bikes (motocross) at the time. So we decided to take our dirt bikes with us on a two-rail, open motorcycle trailer pulled by the Impala. We planned to ride many of the famous California motocross tracks while we were out there.

Earlier that summer, before our trip, Dave and I had met a pair of girls while we worked summer jobs in Gunnison, Colorado. Dave and I and some other high school buddies were building prefab concrete apartments for the college students at Western State College in Gunnison. Dave and I hooked up with Rita and Trisha at a local Gunnison breakfast spot called the Wagon Wheel. We dated the girls all summer long. It turned out that Rita and Trisha were also planning a road trip out west: Arizona, Las Vegas, and then Southern California. Dave and I made plans to meet the girls several times along the way.

Dave and I left Denver in August of 1970. The girls left Gunnison at the same time. We planned to meet first at the Grand Canyon, and that we did. Dave and I camped in a campground on the South Rim. The girls stayed at the El Tovar Lodge on the South Rim. We met them for a fancy dinner at the lodge and then a moonlight stroll along the paths on the South Rim. More than that I will not tell.

Our next meetup was in Las Vegas. Dave and I sprung for a motel room off The Strip. The girls, once again, enjoyed fancier digs at one of the big casino hotels—The Sands perhaps. Again, we met them for dinner and to play the slots in the casino. We parted ways late that night, and Dave and I headed back to our motel room to sleep.

Our final meetup was to be in Los Angeles several days later. Dave and I loaded up the Gray Goose and made sure the radiator and gas tank were full. Stops between Vegas and LA were sparser back then. We made sure that we had extra oil, water, and antifreeze in case we ran into trouble in the Mojave. With all the loading and preparations, we ended up getting a late start from Vegas. We were concerned about the already scorching temperature—nearly a hundred degrees Fahrenheit, even in the morning.

We motored along without trouble. We had the windows fully down, wing-windows swung open to direct a breeze to our faces, enjoying the new sights and chatting about surfing and motorcycles—and the girls, I am sure. We passed through State Line without incident. There wasn't much there in 1970. After State Line, we started up the long inclines that mark the route between the California state line and Victorville. Dave and I kept a close eye on the temperature gauge and the radiator for any signs of overheating. The temperatures outside were now well above a hundred degrees. The Halloran Summit was still in the distance. We stroked the old Impala along. Up ahead, we saw a car with its hood up on the right side of the road. As we approached, we saw that it was the girls' car and that they were standing outside. We pulled over behind them.

I paused my reflection about 1970, and grabbed a Coke from the cooler in the back seat. Cynthia still slept in the passenger seat, and Durango Pete was just as oblivious in the back seat, curled up on his side in his dog bed. I saw the sign for the Halloran Summit ahead. This was near the spot Dave and I had rescued the girls forty-five years back. Time has wings. I popped open the Coke, took a sip of the cold, syrupy drink, and then resumed my daydream.

The girls were happy to see us. They described what had happened. Dave and I had some mechanical knowledge; it didn't sound good. We were sure they had run the radiator dry and had seized the engine. We loaded their bags into the Gray Goose and took Rita and Trisha to Baker, where we could find a phone to call their parents and a mechanic to help with their car. It was a very slow go from there to Baker. Our car was now even more heavily loaded and more likely to overheat—the same as their car had done. We nursed the Goose along, and we made it to the top and then coasted downhill into Baker.

The girls called their folks (I wasn't envious of that call), and Dave and I found a garage to help them. There was a local motel that had a vacancy, so we decided to overnight there with the girls. We wanted to make certain that they were set with help the following day before we went on to Los Angeles. We all spent a fitful night without much sleep, and certainly there was no lighthearted spooning.

The next morning, we had breakfast together. At the garage, we found out that the motor had in fact seized, and the car was not worth fixing. We needed to take the girls on to Los Angeles. Their trip had unceremoniously come to a premature end. They had gotten firm instructions from their parents to catch a flight from LA back to Denver, where their parents would pick them up and return them to Gunnison. The car had to be sold for salvage.

Dave and I got the girls to LA and their flight home, and we completed our big road trip. We camped at Seal Beach and at San Onofre. We hit San Diego, Tijuana, Santa Barbara, Pismo Beach, Big Sur, Carmel, Half Moon Bay, San Francisco, Tahoe, Bonneville, and Salt Lake. We even drove through Sundance, Utah, where we saw Robert Redford with his shirt off, high on a ladder, working on the siding of his mountain home. Finally, we passed through Dinosaur National Monument and Steamboat Springs, Colorado, on our way home to Denver.

In California, we raced our motocross bikes at Indian Dunes, went to the Ontario 500 for the Questor Grand Prix, and surfed at Huntington and Laguna Beach. That is when I fell in love with the old art community that nestles at the base of the coastal mountains south of Newport Beach. I caught my best waves on a glorious day at Laguna in 1970. Over four decades later, I was headed back there in the company of my soul mate and with a crazy cattle dog who had captured my heart too. It had been a great trip in the summer of 1970, with a great friend and two awesome cowgirls from Gunnison, Colorado. On this much later adventure, I had another great trip to anticipate and two travel mates that were as fine as they come.

Cynthia and Pete awakened as we approached Barstow. "Did you guys have a good siesta?" I asked. They both yawned widely, so I guess that was a yes. "You missed a great story," I told them. "About my big California trip back in 1970."

CHAPTER 18

"THOSE WITH SHALLOW SOULS NEVER SWIM IN DEEP WATER."

MR. STEVE & DURANGO L. PETE

I TURNED OFF THE INTERSTATE at Barstow. I needed to stretch my legs, and my stomach reminded me that it was lunchtime. I was certain that my sleepy traveling companions were overdue for a pit stop and chow. "Yep," I said. "You guys sure missed a great story about the old days, surfing, and an old flame of mine."

They both looked at me and then at each other knowingly. "We're hungry, and we need a bathroom break," they said. So much for their love of my storytelling.

In Barstow, we grabbed Pete a hamburger patty at In-N-Out Burger (it has now become a tradition). We all used the stop to take care of bathroom business, and for ourselves Cynthia and I grabbed a sandwich and drink to go. The great American highway beckoned, and the ocean's siren song would not allow us to linger in the desert.

On to Laguna Beach we flew, over Cajon Pass and down Laguna Canyon, until we finally spied the ocean and the main beach just ahead. Pete stood with his front paws on the center console, and he looked out the windscreen at the biggest lake he had ever seen. "Dad! Look at that! Let's go swimming!"

I gave him a big head scritch and said, "No, Pete, let's go surfing now!"

It took Pete some time to adjust to our little apartment. He was used to a bit more room, and the apartment furnace was noisy. Pete doesn't like any snapping, popping, or cracking noises. He had a few restless nights at the start, until his nervous system accommodated to the noises and he realized we would survive the sounds unharmed.

We wasted no time heading to the beach and the surf. We took the Heisler Park trail south and down the long steps past Las Brisas Restaurant, until we landed at the north end of the main beach. Durango Pete headed to the sand immediately. He sniffed everything. It was all new to him. He checked out the washed-up kelp and ocean debris. He dug every hole in the sand that he so desired without any scolding from us. We laughed to see the sand go flying, and we were relieved that people were sparse and that he wasn't covering anyone up.

I led him to the edge of the water, giving him plenty of slack on his leash so that he could enter if he wanted. He kept one eye ahead and one eye out to sea. Every time a breaker crashed onto the beach, he side-hopped and managed to stay just out of the reach of the water. We weren't sure Pete was going to tackle the deeper water, let alone any waves. Then we spied a big piece of driftwood.

We grabbed it from the sand. Pete saw what we were doing. He cannot resist a stick—especially a big stick. We made our way down the beach, past the old lifeguard tower and to the south end of the main beach. Fewer people were there. Of course, Pete jumped up and down, trying to snatch the big stick from our hands.

Cynthia and I kept him on his leash for the first few tosses. And we didn't throw the stick far out—only far enough that Pete would be in the water up to his belly. The big piece of driftwood was more than he could ignore. Out he went into the water, to the end of his leash and up to his belly in the foam. He grabbed the stick with his teeth and he turned, right before a breaker crashed, the jumbled water chasing after him hot on his tail.

"Mom! Dad! Did you see that? I hightailed it out of there before that monster wave got me!" He had a giant grin on his face despite the driftwood that was still in his teeth. "Yeehaw, baby!" he said. I smiled a smile just as big—Cynthia too. It is always a joy to see so much dog happiness. I am certain that I had grinned liked that when I caught my first perfect wave at Laguna Beach over forty years before.

That was all it took. The game was on. After a half-dozen tosses and retrieves, we unhooked Pete from his leash. Now he was free to really explore the ocean. We tried to time our throws so that he would be in the water between breakers, but we weren't always precise. We tossed the big driftwood even farther out. Pete went after it without hesitation. The water was too deep to wade. Pete was now swimming after the stick. He made it to the stick, grabbed it and turned, swimming strongly toward us where we waited, a bit nervous, on the beach. A good-sized swell caught him as he swam. It lifted Pete up and up. His eyes got big! He was not going to let go of that piece of wood. He swam harder, and now the wave was helping him. Pete was surfing! He rode the wave all the way in to where it crashed right behind him, and he scampered up to us with his prize.

"Cowabunga, Pete!" I yelled as he pranced around us, proud of his big ride. Durango Pete was now officially a surf dog, not just a cow dog from Colorado. Pete had discovered yet another bliss of water.

Our days at Laguna became a predictable but satisfying routine. Breakfasts were simple affairs at our apartment: coffee and yogurt. The days outside began with a long walk in Heisler Park and lounging in the sun on the park benches or on the grass, followed by surfing and sand play south of the main beach. By late morning, Pete was ready for a break from the water, and we walked back north to Starbucks for coffee, or up the hill to Urth Caffé, our favorite stop, for a Spanish latte and a pastry. We hung out on the patio, in no hurry to do this or that, and kicked back in the sun like Pete, who dozed on the warm concrete near our feet.

Lunches were also simple—or skipped. A cup of soup or a small salad usually sufficed. Pete, on the other hand, was famished when we got back to the apartment. We fed him his lunch of kibble, canned food, and cheese sprinkled on top. Afterward, we napped on our big, comfortable bed, the ceiling fan turning lazily and blowing the right cool breeze on the three of us as we slept.

Afternoons began at 3 p.m. We gathered our gear and returned to Heisler Park for another walk and more surfing, this time at the beaches located north of down-town Laguna and nearer to our apartment. Pete surfed and explored the tide pools with us, scrambling up on the rocks and then looking out to sea wistfully. When he was good and soaked from surfing, he sprinted up and down the beach and then rolled in the sand with great vigor until he was coated with sticky, wet grains from nose to tail. We laughed and laughed to see his silliness and glee. We weren't concerned about the sand coating that he sported. We had learned long before that Pete is a self-cleaning dog. There is something about his coat that allows him to shake two or three times to make the sand disappear.

Each day ended with a glass of wine and the watching of the sun set over Catalina Island in the distance. We had a good spot, on a grass hill near the north terminus of Heisler Park. Pete and Cynthia lounged in the grass, and I took picture after picture of the water and of the sun falling slowly from the sky. I sat there, fully in the moment, simply being present. On a few occasions, a truth presented itself. I made a mental note, or I took a moment to write it down in my phone journal.

In my doting years, I have become more reflective. When I hike in the mountains or on the high prairie, I do not hurry. I focus on my footsteps. Their rhythm takes me to a place that is expansive in its narrowness. When Pete and I stop, and when we sit on a boulder or a tree stump, I close my eyes. In my stillness, and in my silence, I experience my essence at its core. In these times, I hear the music of creation and the song of the Universe. Sitting by the sea is no different.

Dinner, following the disappearance of the sun on the horizon, became as rote as surfing and walks and napping had become. We dined mostly at one of two favorite dog-friendly restaurants: Lumberyard Restaurant, a local hang-out located east of the main drag, and The Cliff, a more touristy restaurant, but one with a great patio overlooking the main beach and the ocean. Pete liked both restaurants, but he told me that he was partial to Lumberyard because it was a "more honest place," meaning that it was not so full of noisy tourists and that the food was simpler, more familiar to a dog's sensitive palate. The patio at Lumberyard was secluded and quiet. And it had nice benches with cushions that felt just right on a dog's tender paws and backside. Finally, it had propane tableside heaters, and the waitstaff were good about giving Pete plenty of love, his own bowl of cold water on the tabletop, and most of all—his own large hamburger patty, sometimes with cheddar cheese if he was particularly handsome and agreeable.

As the days in Laguna rolled along, we ventured out to other beaches, especially the beaches that were dog friendly and that allowed dogs to be off their leashes. Huntington Dog Beach was the closest.

We enjoyed the thirty-minute drive to Huntington. We took the Coast Highway the entire distance, passing through Corona del Mar and Newport Beach before arriving at the dog beach, located north of Huntington proper. One day, one of many spent there, the weather was stormy. The skies were overcast, and the onshore winds were strong. There was little rain, but the surf was big. The ocean was alive and angry. Even so, many people were on the beach with their dogs. And many of the dogs were cavorting in the shore break and in the foam between the break and the beach. Durango Pete, or The Laguna Kid as I now called him, was eager to be out of the apartment. Clearly, he needed a lot of exercise. He strained at the leash, looking at the water, wanting to get in it—now!

In retrospect, I should have been more cautious that day. I found out later that evening that there had been surf advisories. But I had my own eyes, and I could see that it was a rough day. Anyhow, Pete was exuberant, and we wanted him to get plenty of exercise. We unhooked his leash, and off he went into the ankle-deep water. Sticks were plentiful, washed up everywhere, woody gifts from distant places and a stormy sea. Cynthia and I each grabbed one or two of the larger sticks so that we could keep him going if one piece of wood was sucked out to sea.

The stick and surf play went well for most of the morning. Pete did a little swimming, but he took few chances in the turbulent water. I was glad to see that he was being cautious. Years back, when I lived in California, I had been body surfing at Zuma Beach near Malibu. Zuma was notorious for its riptides. I got caught in a very strong one. I had decided to swim to the beach for a bit of rest from surfing. I started my way in, swimming leisurely. I looked up from time to time, and I noticed that I was being pulled backward, farther and farther from the shore. I swam harder. I looked up again, and I could see that I had made little, if any, progress. I started to get worried. I wasn't that familiar with the ocean back then. I saw two lifeguards running up and down the beach, yelling at several of us in the water and pointing sideways with big, sweeping gestures. Finally, I figured out that the lifeguards wanted us to swim parallel to the beach. I turned and swam north, parallel to the shore. Soon I felt the offshore current release its grip on me, and I swam in to the beach, completely exhausted. I sat down in the sand. The lifeguards were by that time in the water with their flotation devices. They had to rescue several other people who were near where I had been surfing.

Cynthia and I were about to wind up our water session with Durango Pete. I threw an especially large piece of driftwood into the water. Pete was on it! The driftwood was pulled back and to the side. Pete changed directions and went after it. He had no problem swimming to it and grabbing ahold of the log. He turned and started to swim in. But like me so many years ago, he was caught in a backwash and was going backward despite his powerful swimming. I saw his expression change. A big swell had come up behind him, and the backward pull was even stronger. He was headed away from the shore. He dropped the big log, a look of full-on panic on his face. Still, he swam—desperate to come to shore. I waded into the surf up to my thighs, ready to swim after him. The big wave finally broke, right on top of Pete. He was completely swamped. His disappeared from sight—under the broken, sudsy water. But the wave had changed the water's energy. Pete surfaced and started swimming again. He inched closer and closer to where I stood in the water. Cynthia had joined me in the foam. We were both soaked. Finally, Pete reached us and we grabbed him, helping him walk to the beach. We hugged him all over. "Oh, Petey! Are you OK, buddy boy?"

When we let him go, he shook the water off with two or three giant shakes, "Holy crap! I was headed to Hawaii, Dad! Jeesh, I'm tired! Let's go home and get a cheeseburger."

"Anything you want, Pete!"

On our drive back south to Laguna, I thought about our close call with Pete. I hoped that the experience would not spoil the ocean and surfing for him. I thought about how horrible it would have been to have lost Pete. I couldn't imagine.

Durango Pete is a very good swimmer. When he is motivated, he can swim with almost any retriever at the dog park ponds. The wake he leaves behind when he is really motoring in the water is impressive. Pete and I have encountered other cattle dogs in our travels, and in most cases, we discover that they too are good swimmers. As we drove along the coast, I thought about what had happened, and I thought about a fascinating story I had discovered when I was doing my cattle dog research on the Internet, early in our relationship with Durango Pete.

I had stumbled upon a fantastic story about a cattle dog in Australia that swam over five miles through shark-infested waters. Durango Pete is a good swimmer, but I am not sure that even Pete could swim five miles in the ocean.

The incredible story of Sophie Tucker began in November of 2009. Sophie was sailing with her owner, Jan Griffith, and family off the north coast of Queensland. The water was quite choppy that day, and Sophie fell overboard. The family searched for Sophie at length, putting their own lives at risk in the stormy seas. They were unsuccessful in finding their beloved cattle dog. They were certain that she must have perished. Quite the contrary. Sophie survived and started swimming, reaching St. Bees Island, located five to six miles northeast of the Mackay

Coast and far from the point where the family had lost her.

St. Bees Island is inhabited by only a few hundred people. It has dense rainforests and a population of koalas and wild goats. Sophie was spotted from time to time by locals living on the island. They thought she was a feral dog and did not try to capture her or report her presence to authorities.

After a time, though, the carcasses of several baby goats were found. Locals decided to report this to the wildlife authorities. The officials discovered Sophie, and they thought that she might have been killing livestock for food. Word got back to the mainland about a stray dog on St. Bees Island killing young goats. Jan Griffith and the family wondered if it could be Sophie Tucker, but they were dubious. When they heard that the dog was being brought to the mainland, they decided to have a look. It turned out that the St. Bees dog was their Sophie, who had been gone four months. Sophie Tucker was quite happy to see her family. And they were overjoyed to see her!

Local fishermen were incredulous that Sophie had survived her swim. Tiger sharks and hammerheads frequent the water through which she swam. The fishermen said that the smell of wet dog is quite attractive to sharks, and dogs rarely survive for long in the water. Sophie's story is available in the book *Sophie: Dog Overboard,* by Emma Pearse.

Cattle dogs are known for their toughness, hard-headedness, and devotion to their owners and families. Sophie is proof. What about Durango Pete? He is pretty odiferous when he is wet. Would sharks have gotten Pete even if he was a strong swimmer and could have stayed afloat? I didn't want to think about it. And I didn't want to ever find out. I thought, "Yes, Pete—let's get a cheeseburger—and some damned french fries!"

A dog can surprise you; that's for certain. They sneak up on your heart. Cynthia and I kept ourselves busy with all the things humans typically do. We worried over work and income and over the health of our kids and grandkids, and we even worried about our own declining physical capacities. We fixed things around the house that needed fixing. We watered the lawn, shoveled snow, and trimmed the bushes. We picked up groceries and put them away. We paid the bills, vacuumed the floors, and did the laundry. We read the news and stewed about politics and world affairs.

But we had a dog. And dogs also demand certain things. We fixed Pete's meals. We brushed his coat and took him to the vet. We worried when he was sick. We played with him when he was well. We took him on the walks that we knew he needed—for his health and sanity, for our own health and sanity. We napped with him, we dined with him, we traveled with him, and we slept with him. And as I thought about that scary morning in the surf, I knew without a doubt how much I loved Pete. I realized that Durango Pete was a messenger, that he was a facilitator, that he was not simply a receptacle for us. He was not a simplistic animal who depended upon us for everything— for his survival. No. I realized then and there that Pete was a vehicle, a traveling soul with four legs, upon which we had climbed and were now moving forward and into dimensions and an enlightenment that would have been much harder were it not for him. Durango Pete was growing in skills and depth as a soul because he was willing to give us a chance and because he took other chances—like swimming in the rough ocean. We had taken a deep plunge in committing ourselves, not at a young age, to a crazy cattle dog.

Because of Pete, we had climbed out of ourselves. We had learned to listen to him, he who could not speak out loud with a voice and words like ours, but who experienced all the emotions we experienced—joy, fear, hunger, fatigue, curiosity. He had so much to say and so much to teach us. We simply had to invite him to speak. And we had to learn how to be quiet, to give space for his messages and wisdom to reach us.

I thought about all the places Pete had taken us in only four years. As much as we took him, he took us: Tucson, New Mexico, so many places in Colorado, and finally California and Laguna Beach. These trips all had happened because we had wanted good things and experiences for him. Pete was the stimulus for the adventures in this book. And Durango Pete is the vehicle and the avenue through which I have traveled outward and inward. It is because of Durango Pete, and because of those journeys, that I have connected with my own past, with the histories of the places where we walk, with my ancestors, with my own journey, and with my very soul. The musings that start every chapter, the poetry that graces many of these pages, the many short stories I have come to write when Pete and I have been sitting on a rock in the wilderness or on a bench on the ocean boardwalk, I owe to Durango Pete. Yes, Pete has taught Cynthia and me so much about the blessing and the joy of life, the companionship of a dog, and—of course—the simple joy of naps.

Speaking of naps and sleeping, here is a poem that Pete and I wrote one summer evening in Colorado as we sat on our patio enjoying the stars and the moon, being fully in the moment and understanding the brevity and beauty of it all.

Hang the Moon

By Stephen Hinman & Durango L. Pete

What a loving, tender, buttered light
The moon that bathes the summer night
And the souls who slumber in the glow
Soft, in feathered beds below.

Dream, between the stars that rise
The sights seen with shuttered eyes
Clouds that drift on lazy feet
The owl who cries a two-note beat
"Who who☐who who"

Who hears the crickets' sweet refrain
The mournful whistle of a train?
The stars will fade all too soon
And the sun will put away the moon.

CHAPTER 19

"WE FIND AWARENESS IN THE CRACKS AND FRACTURED MOMENTS OF LIFE."

MR. STEVE & DURANGO L. PETE

TRUTH BE KNOWN, THAT DAY when I traveled to the adoption event at Petco with Cynthia and Krista, I wasn't fully ready to bring a new dog into my life. I missed having a dog's companionship, for sure. I did the mental Ben Franklin, listing the positives and the negatives of having a dog in the family again. But that was largely an intellectual endeavor. In my heart, I still was grieving the loss of Pumpkin, who had been with us for eighteen years. Grief cannot be rushed, and it colors the world even when you think it has passed. Pumpkin had colored my dog worldview the way every dog who had been part of my family since the time I was a small boy had done. With the arrival of Durango Pete, I became a four-dog man. I want to tell you a little bit about his predecessors—especially Pumpkin.

The first dog in my life, Snuffy Smith, my childhood dog, passed away while I was off at college. Snuffy was a toy shepherd mix. He had been in my life since I was six years old. I had grown up. Snuffy had grown old. When it was clear that Snuffy was miserable—blind, lame, and sick much of the time—my mother took him to our vet to be euthanized. She could no longer helplessly watch him suffer. My two brothers and I were gone. My dad was not one to watch what had to be done, let alone make the decision to end a life. My mom took care of all the details—without assistance. I don't know how she did it by herself. Old Snuff was her dog without a doubt. He adored my mom, and she loved him no less. He waited for her arrival home from work every night for fourteen years, peering out of our big picture window at the front of the house, his nose resting on the low windowsill. Snuffy was no longer able to even do that. My mom did what was the honorable and loving thing to do—for a dog who worshiped her and whom she loved.

In those days, a dog's remains were not customarily returned to the owners. So there is no resting place where I can visit old Snuff, unless it is the small frame house on Nielsen Lane in Denver where Snuffy and I grew up. There is no small marker to note his resting place, no favorite haunt where his ashes were spread. Perhaps his spirit still roams the backyard on Nielsen Lane, looking for neighborhood kids to harass. Still, despite the passing of nearly fifty years, Snuffy lives on in my memories and in my heart.

Champ, a spunky Yorkshire terrier on the large side, was my second dog. He was the first dog that I owned—if we ever really own them. More likely they own us. Champ died at the age of fifteen on a farm in Paola, Kansas. He plain wore out, old Champ. I lived in Kansas City when

Champ died. Champ lived with my children and their mom on their small farm. I had only been apart from Champ for a few years following my divorce.

The same as Snuffy, Champ grew old while my children grew up. He is buried on the farm, which is no longer in the family. Sometimes I wonder if he is lonely there. We all moved away. All of Champ's humans live in Colorado now. But old Champ—he's still out on the farm in Kansas, buried next to the fence.

Champ was my first four-legged travel companion. He kept me company on trips from Denver to California and Kansas City to Denver and back. He was a great dog. It was a tough few years that surrounded his passing. First, there was my divorce, and then, not long after, Champ passed away. I am sorry to this day that I was not there to say goodbye when he crossed over. I hope he forgives me. I hope he forgives us for not taking him along when we all moved west. He never was much of a farm dog. Like Snuffy, though, Champ lives on in me. He made me a better human.

Finally, before Durango Pete came into our lives, there was Pumpkin. Pumpkin was likely a Manchester terrier/beagle mix. Cynthia and I called her Punky Lou or just Punky. She passed away seven years ago, in Kansas City like Champ. Pumpkin was eighteen years old when she finally crossed over the Rainbow Bridge. I was there, as was Cynthia. She was curled up in Cynthia's arms for her last breath. Pumpkin was the first dog I watched die. At that moment, I remembered my mom, and I knew how it had been for her with Snuffy Smith.

After Pumpkin passed away and we had received her cremains, Cynthia and I sprinkled a bit of Punky Lou here and there. Some of her remains were scattered at our house in Mission, Kansas. We put her in the flower garden, just outside of the big south-facing windows where she loved to lay and sunbathe. We also put her in the park two blocks from our Mission house. We put her next to the park bench where we would sit for a spell on our walks. She loved that park. The rest of her we saved, much to Durango Pete's chagrin, because he knew that some of Pumpkin's ashes rode with us in our car—in a silk purse in our glove box. We didn't want to give her up completely, so we kept the silk purse with us. Even so, we knew that one day soon we would part with the rest of her ashes too. We knew that we needed to take her to the top of Byers Peak in Colorado, a place Pumpkin loved. The time was near for Cynthia and me to have more closure. And we knew that it was now Durango Pete's time to be the star doggy in our lives. He had earned that honor. Pete had been with us for longer than two years, and he was an inseparable part of the family. Sure, we still compared Pete to Pumpkin from time to time even though we tried not to. Each time we mention her name, Durango Pete slinks off muttering to himself, "Pumpkin, Pumpkin, Pumpkin!"

Cynthia and I began planning a trip to the mountains near Winter Park, Colorado, to carry Pumpkin's ashes up Byers Peak. We knew the spot where we would scatter her. Of course, Durango Pete would go with us. We would give a proper send-off to one great dog in our lives, and we would officially recognize that Durango Pete was now carrying on the honorable work that Snuffy, Champ, and Pumpkin had started—shaping me and Cynthia into new, better versions of ourselves.

One day I was sitting at my desk, alternately studying the map of the climbing route up Byers Peak and gazing out the window at cartoon clouds in the sky. Durango Pete was sleeping on his side on the carpet nearby. I remembered that day when Pumpkin was twelve years old and we climbed Byers Peak.

It had been only Punky Lou, Cynthia, and me. We had a fine summer day for the climb. It was one of those days when things conspire in the happiest ways. Punky Lou was still in great shape even though she was twelve years old and sporting a prodigious amount of gray on her muzzle. She had already gotten to ride in the car over Berthoud Pass on the way to the trailhead. We rolled the windows down so that she could put her head out of the car and take in all the great mountain smells and sights. What a smile she had on her face! She kept her head outside the window the entire trip up to the summit of Berthoud Pass, down the other side, and all the way up the long, dirt road that led to the trailhead for Byers Peak. Unlike Durango Pete, Pumpkin loved to ride in the car.

The trail started out on an old logging road. It was only moderately steep. We kept Pumpkin on her leash for the first part of the hike. After a mile and a half or so, the trail became single-track, and the pitch steepened. Once we were on the single-track and in the trees, we took Pumpkin off her leash. She was free to scamper about and to sniff any smell that tickled her dog fancy. She bounded to the left and right of the trail, trying to take it all in—the trail and the entire lodgepole and fir forest. She never ran ahead more than thirty yards. There she waited until we caught up to her; then she did it all again. That is how it went, up the entire mountain, Pumpkin grinning the whole while.

When we had hiked about three miles, the trees became smaller and started to thin. I knew that we were approaching timberline. Shortly, we exited the trees and entered the high alpine terrain of grasses, sedges, and krummholz. The vistas opened. We were surrounded by high peaks in all directions. The upper north ridge of Byers Peak was visible straight ahead. It looked steep, and I could see that there were several false summits along the way. We had another mile and a half of steep climbing to gain the summit. Pumpkin was game for the challenge of the ridge. We continued up the mountain.

While the steep path was no problem for Pumpkin, Cynthia and I were not having such an easy time. Our pace slowed, and we started to use pressure breathing and rest-stepping on the steepest pitches. Little by little, we made our way up the ridge. Our progress was slow, but we moved steadily forward and up. Pumpkin kept us well within her sight.

After an hour and a half of climbing, I spotted the final pitch to the summit. The weather was starting to change. The sun was gone. A blanket of gray clouds had rolled in. The clouds were high enough that they did not engulf the summit, or us. I scanned the horizon in all directions, looking for any signs of lightning. I did not see any threats.

I could see that the final pitch was very steep and would require hands and feet: Class 3 climbing. Cynthia wasn't eager to climb the large talus and boulders on the summit pitch. She decided to hunker down in a grove of krummholz and out of the wind. The temperature had dropped. I put my shell on over my fleece vest. Pumpkin decided to wait in the short, twisted trees with Cynthia. I continued, and in short order, I scrambled up the boulders, and I summited Byers Peak. I snapped a few pictures and then headed back down to where Cynthia and Pumpkin waited. They were both happy to see me. I crawled into their cozy little space in the shrubbery, and we all shared some snacks and water. Pumpkin could have summited too, but she wanted to stay with her mom and make sure that Mom was OK while I was gone. That Pumpkin sure did love her mom.

Pumpkin had as much fun going down the mountain as she had climbing it. When we reached the car at the trailhead, she had done nearly ten miles of hiking. She didn't even look tired. Pumpkin was an amazing endurance dog. But climbing Byers Peak would turn out to be the last long-distance hike or run she would do. Pumpkin still did plenty of four- to six-mile hikes and jogs before she crossed over the Rainbow Bridge. But Byers Peak was the greatest outdoor adventure Cynthia and I had with Punky Lou.

Pumpkin was not a dog to complain. She had a few nicks and injuries over the years. She tore a deep laceration in her abdomen when she tangled with some barbed wire. The vet stitched her up nicely. Pumpkin never once whimpered or nipped at us or the vet. She mostly left the wound and dressing alone. It healed without drama.

On a walk from our house to the park nearby, Pumpkin was attacked by a chow that was roaming free. Pumpkin defended herself. She did pretty well considering she was a seventeen-pound dog. She did suffer a few wounds, but nothing major. Her mom came to her rescue. Pumpkin was on her leash. But it was a retractable leash, and Pumpkin was at the maximum length. Her mom took on the chow, fell, and broke her wrist in the process. Pumpkin was grateful that her mom stood up to the big dog. She took good care of her mom while Cynthia's wrist healed.

The most frightening event with Pumpkin happened one day while Cynthia was at home, working remotely. It was providence that Cynthia was home. We had a house-guest staying with us at the time. Cynthia's best friend, Kim, was visiting from Seattle. Pumpkin was sunbathing near her favorite south-facing windows at the back of our house. Cynthia and Kim were working at the dining room table, near where Pumpkin was sleeping. Suddenly Pumpkin stood up. Then she staggered, trying to walk. Finally, Pumpkin collapsed onto her side. Cynthia and Kim both saw Pumpkin crumple. They knew something major was wrong. They scooped up Punky, hurried to the car, and drove immediately to the emergency animal hospital only a mile from our house. They knew Pumpkin well at the hospital from previous emergency visits. It was a good thing that Cynthia and Kim acted quickly. It was a good thing that the hospital was so near.

Unbeknownst to us, Pumpkin had developed liver cancer. It had been a completely silent process. We had seen no signs that this was taking place. Punky's cancer had resulted in a large hematoma growing on her liver. The cancerous growth had ruptured and caused her collapse near Cynthia and Kim. Pumpkin was quickly bleeding to death. The vets made a fast diagnosis. Emergency surgery was needed. Cynthia told them to do it. Then she called me at work to let me know what had happened.

The surgery went well. The doctors removed a large cancerous mass. And they stopped the bleeding and sutured the problem areas. Pumpkin had survived a very close call. I hurried to the hospital after work to see her. Cynthia met me there. Punky was heavily sedated, and one side of her abdomen was shaved of fur and sported a large surgical bandage. Intravenous lines and other needed tubes ran here and there. We opened her kennel door. She raised her head and looked at us. We saw only love for us—and the stoic resignation that Punky Lou always displayed when she dealt with adversity and pain. She never once complained. She simply survived and advanced. She did it with grace and pure gratitude for the life she loved. She was not yet ready to give up walks to the park, car rides, and snuggles with her mom.

The good news from the doctors was that the liver cancer was of a type that grows slowly. The hope was that Pumpkin would die of old age before the liver cancer would take her. Pumpkin made it through her surgery, survived her recovery in the hospital, and returned home to the house she loved. She came home to her kitty cat brother, Rocky. She came home to her heated dog bed by the south-facing windows. She came home to bring joy to her mom and to me.

Durango Pete rustled about a bit on the floor, letting out a big groan as he rolled onto his back—one of his favorite sleeping positions. I smiled. Then, I returned to thinking about Punky Lou.

Pumpkin and Cynthia had a special relationship. Her mom walked on the moon as far as Punky Lou was concerned. And Cynthia felt the same about her. A dog can change a person. Usually it is for the better. Now, I am not saying that my wife needed improvement. But we are all a work in progress, and Cynthia and I are no exceptions.

In the same way that Durango Pete has been a force for change in my life, Pumpkin brought about change in her mom. And it was all good. Cynthia always said that she would never have made a good mother. She never had her own biological kids. But she was one heck of a good step-mom. And she was a great mom to Pumpkin. I think that little dog helped Cynthia in so many ways. A dog loves you without conditions. That is a good lesson to learn. True love doesn't require one to earn it. It just is. It is given free-ly, with joy and without payment due. It should be received the same way.

Dogs teach you to live in the moment. They don't ap-pear to worry about next week. They don't worry about the mess they are making. They simply have a blast mak-ing it. Perhaps we discover a bit of that dog joy when we make our own messes, when we live in the moment, or even when we watch our kids and stepkids making their little messes and having their own little adventures. Most of the messes clean up pretty well—those made by dogs and kids. The truth is, Cynthia was a lot better about the messes our kids made than I was. Thank you, Punky Lou.

As Pumpkin moved into her old age, I began to worry about what I knew was waiting down the line. Cynthia had never parented a dog before. And she had never lost one to old age and death. The grief of saying goodbye and the profound emptiness in the home that is present after a dog is gone are overwhelming. I began to dread the day.

Old age took its time with Punky Lou. Her teeth be-gan to show the telltale signs of her advancing years. The gray on her muzzle spread until it encircled even her eyes and her brow. The sparkle in her beautiful, brown eyes dimmed, and the clouds of cataracts appeared. I missed the root beer shine of her round eyes most of all. Despite all the outward physical changes, Punky still loved to eat. She still loved to wander at the park near our house. And most of all, she still loved to snuggle with her mom every chance she could.

Right before she turned eighteen years old, Pumpkin began to deteriorate quickly. She started to have problems with incontinence. She started vomiting food too. We had to change her diet. We prepared her meals by hand, using very bland, easy-to-digest foods. Mostly, we fed her a combination of rice and hamburger or chicken. She easily dehydrated. Periodically, we took her into the vet for subcutaneous fluids.

The most disconcerting changes we saw were the onset of anxiety and the fact that she began to separate from us, spending more time sleeping in unusual places and in isolation. Pumpkin began a series of setbacks followed by periods of improvement. Cynthia and I wrestled with the prospect of Pumpkin's death. We struggled with how to know when it was time to help her cross over. We weren't getting clear signs that Pumpkin wanted to leave. It was agonizing for us—not knowing. Every night we went to sleep wondering if Pumpkin would be gone when we awakened. We woke up frequently to check on her. If we couldn't see her breathing, we panicked, desperately looking for signs that she was still alive.

This was how it went for several weeks. To make matters worse, our kitty cat, Rocky, was also turning eighteen years old. Like Pumpkin, he was in declining health. Cynthia and I decided to call an animal whisperer in Colorado, the same one we would later call for help with Durango Pete. We were looking for any help and advice we could get about end-of-life decisions for Pumpkin. We had used the animal whisperer before, with Pumpkin and Rocky on other matters.

The animal whisperer told us that she was not getting a sense that Pumpkin was ready to leave. She talked with us about what to look for in Punky's behavior that would indicate Punky's desire to cross. She encouraged us to tell Pumpkin that, even though we loved her dearly, it was OK for her to leave. Finally, she told us that it is always best if a dog can pass naturally and in its own space. But she said that is not always possible. Finally, she told us that Pumpkin loved us and had experienced a great life. She said that Pumpkin would always be close by.

We had many visits with Pumpkin's vet the last month of Pumpkin's life. The staff and doctors at Mission Med Vet were helpful beyond measure. They had saved Pumpkin on the day her liver hematoma ruptured. They saved Rocky from spontaneous peritonitis and internal bleeding when he was only a kitten. Now they were good to Pumpkin as well, in her old age. And they were supportive of us, Pumpkin's human parents, who were desperate for advice and help. The vet told us that in Pumpkin's current state, she might last two hours or two weeks. As it turned out, our dear Punky Lou lasted two weeks.

On that morning, we awakened and reached for her to see if she was still with us and to give her the hugs, kisses, and love she had earned. She was still alive. But we knew that day was the day. She told us. She told us that she was worn out. She told us that she was tired of the pain and weary of the fight. She told us that she loved her life with us, in our little house in Mission, Kansas. She told us that she loved us. She told us that she knew it was hard for us to say goodbye. She thanked us for letting her go. And then she asked us to help her.

It was a late summer day in September. Cynthia and I called Mission Med Vet and made the appointment to take Pumpkin in for help in crossing the Rainbow Bridge. We called our kids in Denver to let them know what we were doing with Pumpkin. We called Pumpkin's godparents, who lived only a mile from our house in Mission. They said that they would accompany us and Pumpkin to the vet. Not many years before, they had lost their beloved yellow Lab, Target, to a similar cancer. Cynthia and I had rushed up to Mission Med Vet to be with them in their grief and shock. Now it was their turn—to help us say goodbye to Pumpkin.

The rest of that September day we spent lying next to Pumpkin, holding her, kissing her, petting her, and telling her how much we loved her. We thanked her for the love, the light, the laughter, and the joy she had brought to our lives. And we cried. Then—we cried more.

That afternoon, we gathered Pumpkin into our arms. We wrapped her in her favorite cloth blanket, the cream-colored one adorned with doggies and kitties. We told Pumpkin's kitty cat brother what we were doing so that he could say goodbye to her. And then we climbed into the car for the last ride that Pumpkin would take. She curled up in her mom's lap, like she always did in the car.

Pumpkin's godparents were waiting for us when we arrived at the vet. They loved Pumpkin up a whole bunch, the same as they always did, with rubs and kisses. Then they loved her up some more. Finally, they said goodbye to Punky Lou, and Cynthia, Pumpkin, and I were escorted into a room. I sat next to Cynthia and Pumpkin, as close as I could get. Cynthia sat with Pumpkin in her lap and wrapped closely in her arms. Pumpkin's vet kneeled in front of us. She told us how sorry she was that Pumpkin was going to leave us and that she recognized how hard it was to do what we were doing. She told us that it was the right thing to do, that it was the loving thing to do. She told us that Pumpkin would not feel any discomfort. Then she kissed Pumpkin on the nose and gave her some fine scratches on her head.

The term "euthanasia" is derived from "eu" meaning good, and "thanatos" meaning death. Pumpkin had led a good life. She had certainly brought nothing but goodness to our lives. She deserved a good death. She deserved to be free from suffering. Still, we wondered if we were doing the right thing. There is always the nagging doubt about the decision. We felt unsure, despite all the signs and all the reassurances.

Most difficult of all was the simple parting. Though there was nothing much that was simple about it. Pumpkin was family. Every day, for eighteen years, we had slept with her, awakened with her, walked with her, played with her, hugged her, traveled with her, and fed her. In turn, she had nourished our souls and had showered us with her grace and love. How does one say goodbye to such a partner?

How delicate life is. How complicated and simple it is all at the same time. How joyous one moment can be. And the next moment, so devastating that one's stomach is hollowed out. The heart is torn from the chest and laid bare. That is how it was with Pumpkin's passing. All of the years that we had shared with her were condensed into a few seconds, a lifetime traded for a few seconds. A few seconds for us to soak up the warmth of her fur, to feel her familiar shape in our arms, to put our noses into her nape, to smell her perfume, to gaze into her cloudy eyes, to rub her rough paws, to simply treasure the touch of her breath on the backs of our hands and our cheeks. All of this Cynthia and I experienced that last day—until the chemicals reached our beautiful Pumpkin's strong, brave heart. And then—like a puff of wind that shakes a blade of prairie grass—she was gone.

I will save you the wailing and the flood of tears that gushed forth to see her thus. Somehow, we left that room. Somehow, we left the body of our beloved Punky Lou behind. Surely her soul had flown free. We asked her to forgive us for having done such a thing. Then we walked outside into the late summer day.

The sun was already dropping low on the horizon. In our grief, with our eyes stinging from the tears, we looked up at the sky. There, in an opening in the clouds that was the shape of a window, was a rainbow standing on end and stretching from sill to top. Forgiveness and love may be expressed in more than simple words. Cynthia and I knew who sent us that rainbow in a window of clouds. Love does not die with the body. It soars in the heavens. It takes its rightful place in hearts and in the moments of sweet memories, evoked by a smell, or a place, or the light in a fall evening. Love is the reason life exists. It is written in the Scriptures. It is imprinted in our genes. And when and where love has been fully embraced, freely given, and received without condition, not even death has the power for this love to be denied.

CHAPTER 20

"To Truly Connect, We Have to Meet Someone Where They Are— Not Where We Want Them to Be."

Mr. Steve & Durango L. Pete

CYNTHIA AND I WANTED PUMPKIN with us, as she had been for eighteen years. We could not believe she was not coming home with us. Despite the gift of the rainbow she had given us, we wanted to hold her as we had done only minutes before. But that was not possible. Heartbreak and fatigue can give birth to understanding, though.

The rainbow at her passing was not the last message we received from Punky Lou in the days that followed her death. Years before Pumpkin's passing, Cynthia and I had called the animal whisperer to help us with a different concern about Pumpkin. We had called her because we wanted to see if she could tell us anything about Pumpkin's previous owner and circumstances. We knew nothing about Pumpkin's first year or two of life. We wondered whether Pumpkin had been loved or been abused before she had wandered away from her home and we had rescued her.

The animal whisperer told us that Pumpkin had lived with a "round woman" and that when Pumpkin was a little puppy, she used to sleep curled up in the crook of the round woman's elbow. But the round woman did not live alone. She lived in a small, old house with two men. The men were not always nice to the round woman, and there was much yelling and fighting in the house. Pumpkin loved the round woman, but Pumpkin didn't like the two men, and they were mean to Pumpkin as well.

One day, when Pumpkin was older and no longer a puppy, she wandered away from the round woman's house through a gate that was left open. If there was one thing that Pumpkin loved to do, it was to wander and sniff all the wonderful and interesting smells. She was simply doing that which was her nature. Before long, Pumpkin had wandered quite a distance from the round woman's house, and she wasn't sure which way was home. But the animal whisperer told us that Pumpkin hadn't been sad about being lost. Pumpkin might have wandered away in search of a better home. I like to think that she picked us that day.

Given that Pumpkin loved to sniff all things odiferous, and that she sometimes wandered away from our own house, it was not hard to imagine that the Country Club Plaza in Kansas City had been close by and quite appealing as she wandered away from the round woman's house. The smells from the restaurants would have been a siren call to Punky Lou. She lived for food, and she loved to eat. There were also interesting smells coming from The Body Shoppe. The fragrant soaps, lotions, oils, and perfumes would have led Pumpkin there eventually. That is where we found her. That is where Cynthia convinced the shop owner to allow us to take the little dog home with us—the one who had wandered into the shop that morning.

The day we took Pumpkin home from the shop on the Plaza was only a few days from Halloween. Our new small dog was black, with orange and tan markings. Cynthia and I asked our kids who were with us that day what we should name our new dog. The kids said, "Pumpkin."

A day or two after Pumpkin's passing, Cynthia and I wanted to visit The Body Shoppe in the Plaza, where we had first seen her. I also wanted to drive around the neighborhoods surrounding the Plaza, to see if we could figure out where Pumpkin had lived with the round woman. Cynthia and I thought that Pumpkin's house had to be close to the Plaza. I had gotten some visual images about the house in my head. The house was not large. In my vision, it was an older frame house. It had a rundown chain link fence surrounding the yard. The house was weary looking. I thought that if we drove around, I might be able to find the round woman's house.

The Plaza sits on the northern edge of Brush Creek, which is bounded on both sides by Ward Parkway, a very busy street. The homes to the south of the Plaza, to the south of Ward Parkway and Brush Creek, are large, old mansions. It is an area of great wealth. This did not fit with my images or the descriptions of Pumpkin's home that the animal whisperer had depicted. In addition to this, Pumpkin would have had to cross four lanes of fast-moving, heavy traffic, and she would have had to cross Brush Creek. I ruled out the south side of the Plaza as a location for the house. To the east, there were many large, old apartment buildings. Once again, the homes were much too large and made of brick and stone. These homes were separated from the Plaza by Broadway and Main. These streets were two more very busy streets. So I eliminated the east side of the Plaza too.

Traveling west from the Plaza, there was a mix of apartments, businesses, parking garages, and eventually, homes. The homes were located west of Roanoke Parkway, another very busy four-lane trafficway. The homes were smaller than those located east and south, but I didn't believe Pumpkin had lived west of the Plaza.

That left the area to the north of the Plaza. I really believed that Pumpkin's house was located on the hill looking down on the Plaza from the north. There were no major streets that Pumpkin would have been forced to cross. The homes were smaller, and many of them were older frame homes showing the wear and tear of the years. It was a working-class neighborhood. Pumpkin had not wandered off from an advantaged situation. Finally, the trip would have been downhill, and it would not have taken her long to reach The Body Shoppe. Pumpkin was adept at taking the path of least resistance.

After Cynthia and I visited The Body Shoppe, Cynthia got behind the wheel and drove. I wanted to be able to concentrate on the streets and neighborhoods. I was focused. I hoped to receive some sort of "vibe" that would lead me to Pumpkin's old house, the round woman's house.

Up the steep hill we drove from the Plaza shops, heading to the north. Once we had passed the first few streets of apartment buildings, we were into a neighborhood of small homes. I looked left and right, scanning the streets and houses. We had gone a half-mile when I told Cynthia, "Turn left!" She turned. I was certain that we were on Pumpkin's street. Halfway down the block I spotted a small, dreary, white frame house. The paint was yellowed. Clearly, the house had not received much care and upkeep for some time. The trees and bushes were overgrown. The yard was surrounded by a rusty chain-link fence. I spotted a crooked gate to one side of the house. It was hanging precariously by two rusted, old hinges.

"This is it!" I told Cynthia.

In my mind's eye, I could see Pumpkin loafing around the backyard, sniffing the base of the fence as she went. Finally, she arrived at the old gate that had not been closed properly. Out she wandered, following her nose. It wouldn't have taken her long to reach the Plaza. She wouldn't have had to cross any difficult streets. She wasn't particularly worried. It wasn't Pumpkin's nature to worry about much of anything. She was unflappable.

Cynthia and I sat looking at the house for a long time. Then we drove home in silence to our house five miles distant. We dreaded entering with Pumpkin gone. But we knew we had to. It was odd to be in the house with only Rocky there to greet us. We were excited about the prospect that we had found the round lady's house—Pumpkin's house. But we were terribly sad that Punky Lou would not greet us when we got home.

When we entered the house, Cynthia stopped and looked at me. "Steve, do you smell flowers?" she asked me. I sniffed the air. By God, I did smell flowers! I looked around. We had no bouquets.

Cynthia looked me in the eyes. Her own eyes were round with amazement. "Steve, there are no flowers in the house," she said. "I smell gardenias. Pumpkin's fur always smelled like gardenias! Remember? I always told Pumpkin that her fur smelled like gardenias."

I smelled the familiar fragrance too. It was clearly Pumpkin's smell. She was letting us know that she was all right, that she was still around, that she was thankful for her life with us, and that she was thankful for her home in Mission. Most of all, she was telling us that she loved us for setting her free. What a dog. Cynthia and I held each other. We cried and cried—and smiled. Then we cried some more. We missed that little black-and-orange dog more than we could bear.

It was so odd, coming home to a house without Pumpkin. Each time we left to run errands and returned home, we expected her to greet us at the door. This went on for some time. We had gathered up most of her belongings and donated them to local rescues and friends with dogs. A few things we could not part with, mostly her collection of collars. Pumpkin was a bit of a fashionista when it came to collars. Or perhaps we were spoiled by her and loved to dress her up in a new collar from time to time.

Pumpkin's brother, Rocky the cat, missed her too. When they were young, they played together all the time. Rocky chased Pumpkin through the house. Around and around they went at breakneck speed, across the great room, through the kitchen, and into the dining room, and then they would do it again and again. They loved to nap together. Most days, I could find them curled up like cinnamon buns next to each other on the guest bedroom bed. It was a bright, sunny place to nap in the afternoons. And they could be close to their mom as she worked from home at the big desk on the opposite wall.

Later in life, as they both aged, the roughhousing and games of chase stopped. Pumpkin sometimes got short-tempered with Rocky, especially where food was concerned. But I never doubted that they still loved each other.

After Pumpkin died, Rocky began to decline as well. We were still grieving over Pumpkin's passing. Three months after Pumpkin's death, we lost our kitty cat of eighteen years, Rocky M. Hinman. On a cold January night in Denver, Cynthia and I bundled up ourselves and Rocky. Cynthia and I were visiting our kids in Denver at the time. We had brought Rocky with us; he was too sick to leave in Kansas. I was administering subcutaneous fluids several times each day for his dehydration problems. That night, Rocky had told Cynthia and me that he was too tired to continue the fight. He told us that he wanted to join his sister, Punky Lou, on the other side.

We drove through the snow to Deer Creek Animal Hospital, located near the mountains for which Rocky was named. This time, I held Rocky in my arms as the drugs were administered. I will tell you, and I am not ashamed to say this, when he was gone, when he was laying in my lap and arms, his beautiful eyes frozen in a stare and his little mouth open in midbreath, my grief poured out. The sobs and tears came in gushes and torrents. I was surprised by the depth and intensity of my grief. Losing both of our furry family members in such a short time was simply too much. As Cynthia and I left the hospital arm in arm, the snow began to fall. It floated down in giant, soft flakes—bright white and wet in the darkness. They were as white as Rocky's fur and as wet as his pink kitty cat nose. They do send us messages, our beautiful furry companions. They do.

We spread Rocky's ashes in the small garden outside our dining room windows in Mission. He joined Pumpkin there, where we had spread part of her ashes. They both loved those south-facing windows so much. We spread the remaining ashes in the middle of three large boxwood bushes in our backyard garden in Mission. Rocky loved to explore the backyard whenever we let him out with us to do some gardening. He always ended up hiding in the middle of the big boxwoods. It was a fitting place to let him rest.

It was September as I sat at my desk in our house in Denver and remembered Pumpkin and Rocky. Durango Pete was sleeping on the floor near me, on his back and with his paws in the air. It was three years after Pumpkin had died, and a little less than three years since Rocky had passed away. I knew that summer was coming to another end, and fall was awaiting its golden entrance.

Fall is beautiful in Colorado, but snow is always a possibility. In the mountains of Colorado, winter comes very early. Pumpkin's remaining ashes were still riding around with us in our car. We had them secured in a beautiful, tightly woven cloth sack. It was placed in a silk purse and closed with a thin ribbon of green that was tied in a neat little bow. Cynthia and I knew that it was time to take Pumpkin to her favorite place. It was time to go for another long walk in the mountains with Punky Lou. We wanted to relive that wonderful summer day we had spent on the trail with her years before. We wanted to take her up high where she could see for miles and miles, where she could look across the Fraser River Valley to Berthoud Pass. We wanted to place her at the base of the krummholz grove where she and Cynthia had rested and been protected from the wind while I had completed the climb to the summit. This is what Cynthia and I planned to do. But as often happens, life and events have a way of disrupting even the most earnest of plans.

Cynthia's mom had been in a slow decline in Kansas City for the previous year or two. The pace of her deteriorating health had quickened in the previous three months. In fact, we had made an emergency trip to KC in July. Her mom had failed to awaken one July morning. When the staff at the assisted living home could not waken her, she was taken to St. Joseph Hospital. She was in a coma.

By the time Cynthia and I arrived at the hospital from Denver, her mom had awakened, and a multitude of tests were being done in an attempt to find out what had caused her coma. Test after test came back negative. The doctors determined that she had an infection of some sort, perhaps respiratory. Intravenous antibiotics were administered for several days. She was also dehydrated, so IV fluids were started and continued for the duration of her hospital stay.

When Cynthia and I had first arrived, her mom had been very confused. That was not unusual, though her level of confusion during our first few visits was more severe than what we typically saw. As she began to eat again, and recover, she became much more lucid. Cynthia had some great one-on-one time with her mom. I also had the chance to spend most of an entire late morning and early afternoon with my mom-in-law. The time Cynthia and I spent with her mom turned out to be such a blessing. Cynthia's mom would be gone in less than two months.

Cynthia got the call from her brother on an early September day; her mom had passed away in her sleep. She was ninety-one years old. She was a delightful lady. She had a tender heart—a loving heart. Life had not always been easy for her. Her parents were both deaf, and money had been tight. She had suffered her own health issues as a child and had undergone many painful eye surgeries. As a child and an adult, she was shy and not confident. She was prone to anxiety. It was always hard for us to see her worry about so many things. She would not have to suffer or worry any longer, but Cynthia and her brother and sister had lost their last parent. It is always hard to say goodbye and to start your next chapter without your guiding star.

After Cynthia and I had traveled to Kansas City for her mom's funeral services and we had returned to Denver, it was the middle of September. We decided that it was time to take Pumpkin's remains to Byers Peak. We had to hurry to do it before the snow started to fly. It's a difficult thing to lose your mother. I had lost my mom five years prior to that. I knew that Cynthia was hurting. I hoped that it wouldn't be too much to scatter Pumpkin's remains so soon after the death of her own mother. Cynthia assured me that she wanted to go. We contacted Pumpkin's godmother, Kristen, to let her know we were going to climb Byers Peak with Pumpkin's ashes. We wanted Kristen to come. She did—all the way from New Jersey, where she was taking care of her own mother.

We picked a fine day in the third week of September for our trip to Byers Peak. Of course, Durango Pete was going with us. This was going to be a big day for all of us. We were all embarking on a big adventure, and we knew that we had an important job to do. Cynthia and I would be closing the chapter in our lives that belonged to Pumpkin. We knew that once we placed Pumpkin's ashes on Byers Peak, the new chapter—the chapter that was Durango Pete—would be official. Durango Pete knew only that he was going on a car ride in the mountains and that such a car ride usually meant that there would be a ramble in the great outdoors and that it would be another delicious adventure.

It would be good to be up high. Cynthia and I had done many climbs over the years. We loved to be in the thin air and in the alpine landscape where we had to tread lightly. Like us, the plants up high are tender. We knew that the tundra would be in its fall splendor, draped in colors of rusts and yellows and reds, and we knew that the aspens would still be golden. I looked forward to air that would be clear and crisp, the climb that would be good for stretching legs and lungs, and reflection that would be about all that had happened in only a few years. Life had recently dealt both of us many blows. The ax marks were clear. When one lives long enough, the scars are acknowledged, for even the rock bows before the wind. Cynthia and I knew that through hardship some things are gained. One needs to feel the rough edges that have been carved, and through that pain receive awareness and wisdom that cannot be known only through comfort. We knew that we had to look for Cynthia's mom, Pumpkin, and Rocky where they now lived: everywhere. We knew that then, with honesty, humility, and love, we might move forward with grace and be richer and stronger in our own fabric.

A Covenant

By Stephen Hinman

A rainbow set upon a cloud
Resting on a promise made.
The lowering sun wandered by
Casting scattered shade.

Afternoon clouds gather up in angry walls
Pregnant, tears will fall.
I hear the slap of shattered drops
That die in evening squalls.

The earth cries out, parched with dust
And drinks from spreading pools
Formed from the tumbling sacrifice
Of tiny, liquid fools.

The trees stand in silent wait
Reach out with branching hands
For the wind that rouses sleeping souls
Cannot deny the heavens' plans.

And I who make my way along
An unfamiliar path

Stumbling in the rain and wind
Will not escape the evening's wrath.

Round and round, and round we spin
The dance that never ends.
We dancers tumble, buried there
Where the dance begins.

Cover us low, with dust and dirt
Wetted by our forfeit sweet
And place a marker at our heads
And a rainbow at our feet.

CHAPTER 21

"It Only Takes a Drop of Sunshine to See Even the Saddest Flower Smile."

Mr. Steve & Durango L. Pete

THERE ARE SOME ADVANTAGES TO age. With age comes perspective. That vision comes at a price. Most things of value do. Knees are sacrificed for experience. Innocence gives way to insight. Seasons come and go, as do people and pets. Each season is to be savored. Each is an ending—and a beginning. Often, one cannot say hello without first saying goodbye. This is how it was with the passing of Cynthia's mom. This is how it was with Pumpkin Lou and Durango Pete. Cynthia and I had said goodbye to her mother. Cynthia and I needed to say our final goodbye to Punky Lou so that we could say hello to Pete in full fashion and with hearts wide-open. Pumpkin and Cynthia's mom would never be forgotten. Forgetting loved ones cannot happen when those who have crossed over and those who we have loved are free to be the butterflies who appear when we least expect them and who—like a flower—always bring a smile to our faces.

Yes, each season is to be savored. Fall in the high country is to be cherished. It is as sweet as it is short. September up high is the morning light splintered into a thousand dancing beams that are sprayed from willows coated with an early frost. Fall in the high country is a sky so blue that your heart soars at the sight of a color so impossibly royal and aches with the understanding that such a color will not last. Just as fall must be sacrificed so that winter can live, skies of turquoise give way to those of slate. But for a moment, the aspen leaves hum with delight at being kissed by the golden sun. So complete is the brotherhood of the aspen with the sunlight that in the golden beam its leaves become a thousand tiny yellow hands waving with joy at the tickle and tease of the smallest breeze.

On just such a day, with Pumpkin's ashes tucked safely away and with Durango Pete—two years old and fully grown—excited to hike in the clean mountain air, we headed into the high country to climb Byers Peak. The sky was as blue as a cornflower, just as it had been the morning of the climb with Pumpkin ten years before.

Cynthia and I have gotten less punctual in our season of maturity. A start to the journey that should have begun at seven in the morning slipped away to 10 a.m. By the time we had finally turned off US 40 at the town of Fraser and covered the seven miles of dirt road to the trailhead, it was noon. A smattering of puffy white clouds had begun to gather overhead. I knew that such a late start meant that summiting the peak was not going to happen. I was only slightly disappointed. It was more important that we get above timberline, to where the krummholz groves were located, the place where we would gently lay Pumpkin Lou

to rest. Durango Pete was as eager as I was to be under-
way. He ran his leash to the end of its full ten feet, keeping
the lead tight as a clothesline, and he looked back at us
with a touch of disgust. "Let's go!" he said.

We had daypacks to stuff with food, water, hats, jackets, and gloves. Cynthia packed Pumpkin's remains in a
small zippered pocket in her pack. The pretty satin sack
with the green bow fit just right. I grabbed my trekking
poles, and finally, off we went. Durango Pete took his position in the lead, as Pumpkin Lou would have done.

A ramble is always a bit like life—a metaphor on foot.
We departed the trailhead in our infancy. Everything we
encountered was new and unique. Roots, rock ledges, and
the path that tilted upward were encountered with legs
rested and strong. The eye was not yet jaded. The repeti-
tion of the tall, thin, scaly lodgepole pines was a delight.
They were a large-numbered family—thin woody citizens
of the montane forest, watching in happy approval as we
passed through. During the trip back down, their dominance would become wearisome.

The trip up is always longer because of the frequent
stops made by us and Durango Pete. Time passes more
slowly going up, as it does when we are young, when childhood warps time, and the intervals between holidays, and
the passing from grade to grade, seems to take forever.
Early in a ramble, we are playful children, with skin alert to
molecules of air moving, with ears that prick to the sound
of whispers heard drifting between the pines. There is a
new flower to peruse, an interesting smell to sniff. There is
rough bark to touch, mountain chickadees that serenade
us with their happy *beeps* and who delight us with their

undulating, rollercoaster flight from tree to tree. Or there is sometimes simple silence to reflect upon. All of it is cherished and profound.

I realized at that very moment—as we climbed higher through the forest—that we are not dogs, or humans, or trees, or birds, or even the brook splashing below. We are all brothers and sisters in molecules and atoms and particles that spin and vibrate in the same space, a magic space that is blue, and green, and sometimes golden and white, a space where willows wave a greeting with thin, woody arms, with fragile fingers of mustard and red the color of rouge. We are the notes required to make the symphony whole. And I realized that if we traveled far enough within, we would see that we all are mostly space—the same space upon which we gaze, where the willows and lodgepoles and chickadees and Durango Pete dwell, all of them no different than I. We would discover that we are a vibration, each of us our own unique thrum. Finally, we would know that the vibration that is us is energy and that death is an illusion because energy cannot be destroyed. Our vibration simply changes. That is how Pumpkin sent the beautiful messages to Cynthia and me when she crossed over. She never really left us. They never do.

Like an adolescent, midway through the ramble up the peak I became eager—impatient even. I yearned for the freedom of timberline, where the forest thins and the sky opens to reveal the lofty summits that still hold patches of the past winter's snow. I was growing tired of being watched and guarded by trees. The open spaces high up offered change and excitement, even a tinge of danger where the path crosses granite ledges that skirt the yawning abyss of cirques, avalanche paths, and plunging couloirs. Then, finally, there is the joy of tundra—surprising in its diversity and complexity, fragile, yet admirable, in its tenacity that allows it to grow in carpets of green and that brightens a landscape otherwise hard and difficult.

When we reached timberline, Durango Pete clearly was as glad to be free of the forest as I was. He ran ahead of us, covering a section of trail as steep as an escalator in a matter of seconds. Then he turned and sprinted back down to where we labored for air and good footing, spraying us with gravel when he performed a perfect hockey stop. His ears were laid back and his lips were stretched into a silly grin.

"Did you see that, Dad? Yeehaw, baby!" he yelled.

We saw it, for sure. And we couldn't help but smile too, to see such dog joy at being outside, up high and free. We smiled too because that is exactly what Pumpkin did. Pete's smile was exactly how she smiled, and his exuberant joy at being free of the trees, where you can see forever, was exactly how she was when she was in the very same place ten years before. I smiled at Pete because a decade before, when Pumpkin was with me, I would have run down the trail in the same fashion as Pete, boots glissading on the gravel and scree and sliding to a similar stop. And like Pete, I would have hollered, "Cynthia! Did you see that? Yeehaw, baby!"

A quarter mile after we exited the forest at timberline, we reached the stands of krummholz right below the steep pitch leading to the first false summit. The sun was gone, lost behind the billowing clouds that had rolled in silently and steadily from the south. I looked around, slowly doing a full turn, to see in all directions, examining the sky for signs of lightning. The ridge upon which we stood would not be a fun place to be during an electrical storm. I saw no flashes glancing off the distant summits and ridges. I heard no thunder. Even so, that could change in an instant. It was too late to continue higher up. The place where we had paused would have to be Pumpkin's resting place.

Cynthia and Kristen explored the krummholz, looking for a good place, one that was protected and out of the wind and a place with a view to the east where Pumpkin could see the morning sun rising from behind James Peak in the distance. I wanted to find a place where the sun would shine on Pumpkin all day as it made its way west through the southern sky.

Cynthia called to me, "I think I have found the place! Come and look."

I wandered over to where Cynthia had knelt in a semi-circular recess, on the east side of a large stand of krummholz. Durango Pete was busy exploring the entire stand of stunted, bushy pines, also known as "knee timber" for their short, deformed growth. The spot Cynthia had found was perfect. I suggested that we should have our lunch on Pumpkin's porch of alpine grass. Then we would conduct a small ceremony in Pumpkin's honor and light some sage we had brought along to bless Pumpkin's new home. The sun decided to slip from behind the clouds to warm our humble spread and Pumpkin's spectacular new home. Of course, when Pete caught wind of food, he came moseying over to see what delicacies might appeal to his cattle dog's fine culinary sensibilities. Durango Pete is nothing if not well-fed.

When all of us had finished our peanut butter sandwiches, cookies, and kibble, Cynthia pulled out the delicate sage and Pumpkin's satin pouch with the green satin tie. We each, in turn, held the pouch and carefully sprinkled some of Pumpkin's ashes onto the bare ground at the base of the krummholz. Durango Pete watched respectfully from nearby. Lighting the sage was tricky in the breeze. But after several efforts—with Kristen and me providing a windbreak—Cynthia was successful. The pungent odor of the sage made its way to our noses. Durango Pete was onto it as well, his ears standing at full attention, his nose high in the air, nostrils wiggling, and his tail pointed straight to the patch of blue sky above our gathering. We each said a brief goodbye to sweet Pumpkin Lou, and then the ceremony was complete.

It's hard not to linger up high when the weather cooperates. We did just that—for a bit. I suspect that it was in part, too, because of our difficulty in leaving Pumpkin. As I said before, and as anyone who has had a pet companion knows, you never really leave them, and they never leave you. Pumpkin was as indelibly imprinted on our hearts and our souls as the color of our hair was imprinted on our genes. If Durango Pete was hoping that the spreading of ashes would fully close the chapter that was Pumpkin Lou, he would be disappointed. Even so, the climb to the high place on the flank of Byers Peak and the spreading of Pumpkin's ashes were as cleansing as the thin, bracing air. And those actions were as good for our hearts as the placing of one foot in front of the other on a forest path that tilts skyward and aims for the blue heavens far above. We had done what we had promised Pumpkin. We had done what we had promised ourselves.

The trip down was typical—reflective. It always is. If the trip up was playful and exuberant, the trip down the mountain was quiet, if not somber. If the trip up was a metaphor for infancy and youth, the trip down was equally metaphorical for the sensibilities that come with maturity and age. It was certainly true that my old knees and hips, which had not yet been replaced, started to protest. The light was fading, and thus the forest was shadowed and deep with a late, filtered light that was shared with us by the weary sun, which now rested on the mountain's shoulder. I resolutely put my sore feet to the descending trail. I had to pay attention. Roots and rocks were eager to catch my feet unaware. I knew from experience that falling at my age had consequences much more severe than when I was younger.

Durango Pete was not weary at all. And he was clearly not in a somber, reflective mood. He was acting up. Two years of experience with him on the trail had taught me not to expect Pete to be calm and cooperative on the return trip. No signs of maturity or reflective wisdom were being manifested in the cattle dog tethered to me by his lead. He was now ripping small bushes from the ground next to the path and breaking branches of considerable size from the lower limbs and trunks of trees adjoining our route. Of course, these became weapons to whack against our legs as he ran by us at full speed. When no appropriate bushes or sticks were available, he turned to biting the leash and shaking his head side to side in a game of one-sided, unwelcome tug-of-war. Pumpkin Lou would never have behaved that way. But we come into the world largely who we are—man and dog—and Durango Pete was—well—Durango Pete.

That is how we wound our way down Byers Peak, in reflection followed by mayhem, until his cattle dog crazies had passed and he returned to sniffing this, that, and the other. Finally, Pete resumed behavior that was easier on us and more appropriate in honoring his well-behaved predecessor, Pumpkin Lou. I couldn't help but smile—and even chuckle a bit—to see Durango Pete's pure joy at being outside, surrounded by a landscape full of wonder, walking with his human pack, and bumping my legs with his nose every few hundred yards so that he could get another dog biscuit.

The trip for Cynthia was important in another big way. Her mother had only been gone a week. Cynthia was using the climb and the time surrounded by the wild places that she loved so much as her own catharsis—or at a minimum, a way to begin the healing journey that all of us must take when we say goodbye to a parent. I cannot know what emotions or memories Cynthia experienced that day. Grief is a solitary journey, despite our own loved ones still present who hold our hands and wipe away our tears.

I have had my own experiences with the profound loss of both my father and my mother. I knew that when your heart is laid so bare, when your soul yearns for some sort of explanation of why we must part with those who gave us everything, and when you surrender to the process of moving forward, sometimes the departed—the way Pumpkin had—send us a sign that they are OK on the other side. There is no knowing that it will happen. There is no knowing when it might happen. And there is no knowing what the sign will be. There is only the knowing that when it happens, that in fact, it is what it is.

Butterflies are significant in times of great change. We had only seen one or two on our trip up the mountain and none halfway on our trip down. But as we walked down the mountain trail in late September, a beautiful blue butterfly appeared. It singled out Cynthia, and it danced about her head. We stopped. After its long beautiful dance, the butterfly landed upon Cynthia's hand. There it remained. Cynthia looked at it in amazement. It rested there, on the back of her hand, as easily as it would on milkweed or the blossom of a rabbitbrush.

After five minutes had passed, Cynthia resumed walking. We did as well. The butterfly remained on her hand, and it became a hitchhiker—a beautiful blue passenger riding on Cynthia's hand as we descended the mountain. It traveled with us for ten additional minutes. Then, as we neared our car, it said goodbye, and off it flew to wherever it was called to or simply wanted to be. Cynthia knew who it was. She knew who had sent her a message, "Don't worry, my dear daughter. Look! I am still here. I sent you a friend so that you would know."

Messages
By Stephen Hinman & Durango L. Pete

Wind chimes and butterflies
My mother sings
And she dances to me on gentle breezes.

We reached the trailhead and our car just as the sun slipped behind the peak for another day. Pete sat down on his haunches in the dirt next to the car, and he looked at us and smiled a big, Durango Pete, chocolate-lipped smile. "Thanks, Mom and Dad. That was great! Hey—what's for dinner? What are we gonna do tomorrow, guys?" he said, firing the questions at us in rapid order. Pete is not the most sensitive soul. He is a hungry and energetic one.

I pulled his dog bowl out of the trunk and filled it with his favorite food. Cynthia poured him a dish of fresh, cold water. We gave him a few leftover dog biscuits and our last chunks of cheese in his bowl. Cynthia, Kristen, and I watched him eat. It had been a good day. The butterfly visit had tied up all the loose ends in a beautiful, blue gossamer-winged bow. I was thankful for this life we had been given and for all of our loved ones past and present.

Durango Pete finished his meal and hopped into the back seat of the car. Down the mountain road we drove in the alpenglow, in the last light of the day, when the sun would finally rest and the moon and stars would rise to watch over us. I was looking forward to climbing into our comfortable bed at home. But despite my tired, sore legs, I was already thinking about what trail Pete and I could explore the following day.

Yes, Durango Pete was never to be underestimated. He was not one who would tolerate neglect, benign or otherwise. He was certainly Pumpkin Lou's match when it came to smarts. They both got what they wanted. But so did we. Pete loved to ramble in the woods the way Pumpkin had. But Pete had a mischievous intellect that Pumpkin did not. Pete had a rambunctiousness, a goofy sense of humor, and a wild, elemental energy that made us smile, even when we were sad. Whereas Pumpkin had been quiet and serious, Durango Pete was loud and fun-loving. His sense of humor and joy of life were infectious. We couldn't help ourselves. It had taken some time, but Cynthia and I had caught the joyous, crazy disease that was life with a little cattle dog who had a big attitude. Bless you, Durango Pete, for bringing smiles to us when our hearts were broken.

Darkness gently dropped its inky curtain on us as we drove down the mountains toward Denver. Pete was as tired as us now, and he slept most of the way home. We enjoyed the quiet and the dark pines slipping by us. Pete finally stirred, and he sat up in his seat as we drove past Idaho Springs.

"Hey, buddy boy," I said. "What's up, Pete?"

"I think I smell a McDonald's, Dad. I could sure use a cheeseburger," he replied, nose in the air and nostrils wiggling. "Hold the pickles and fries, though," he said matter-of-factly.

We looked at each other, and we laughed and laughed. Yes, Durango Pete, our crazy, wild, rodeo cow dog, was well on his way in shaping us, his two-legged companions, into the people he wanted us to be. As for Pumpkin Lou and those we love who are recently and long since passed? Well, they remind us from time to time that they have not forgotten us. Each message is a gift that warms our hearts and brings a smile to our faces.

AFTERWORD

DURANGO PETE IS NOW FOUR and a half years old. Soon he will be five. It is hard to believe so much time has passed since we first met. Our initial trials and tribulations have receded. That is not to say there are no challenges with Pete, even today. He is, after all, a cattle dog. But even though he has become "settled in," he still expects a lot from us. That's OK. He still makes us smile and laugh every day. His vocabulary (which is large) continues to grow. His list of tricks is ever expanding. He gets around as nimbly as he did when he was one. I wish that I could say the same for me. Oh, my vocabulary is still pretty good, and I have a few tricks up my sleeve for an old guy. But the rheumatiz and the Jimmy Leg Syndrome have taken a toll, and our walks have slowed down, and a few of the more challenging off-trail rambles have been suspended—temporarily, I hope. Most likely, there are a few more surgeries and joint replacements coming up soon. It's funny to think about that. Old Jerry, the owner and jack-of-all-trades at Casa De Caballo in Tucson, had commented one day when I was taking young Pete out for another ramble on the ranch (the third of the day), "By God, Steve! I swear you're gonna wear that dog out!" I remember thinking, "No, Jerry. Pete's gonna wear ME out!"

Funny thing; Jerry was fighting prostate cancer at the time. Even so, he was a force of nature. He worked on that ranch from dawn to dusk. I wondered how he did it—how he kept on going. After I was diagnosed with bladder cancer, I thought about him a lot. People come into our lives for a reason. My mother and Jerry and my Grandpa Bill showed me how to face adversity with grace, with a sense of humor, and with a patient toughness and a certain resignation and faith. I would try to do the same.

As I thought about my mom, Jerry, and my Grandpa Bill, I thought about my path. When we are young, we are told to walk the straight and narrow, and we are told to think things through and to make good decisions. Well, truth is, we are largely on an amusement park ride, so it is best to buckle up and enjoy the trip. I thought about Durango Pete and his path. How could he have known that he would end up in Colorado hanging out with a worn-out old poet? How could I have known that I would end up hanging out with a crazy cattle dog the color of cookies and cream who would be named after a town and a man?

I won't pretend to speak for Pete. He can answer that question himself. As for me? I know this: a dog can teach you a lot of things about life and love. In being who they are, they reveal who you are. Every day, Pete walks his path, and I walk mine. From a distance, an observer would say, "I see that man and his dog walk the same path." Yes, our path looks as if they are one. But I know that Pete rarely traces my footsteps, nor I his. It is the journey that we have in common, and I know that there will be a moment, when I am seventy-two years old, that he will have caught me in years, and we will both wear the scars, and the gray hairs, and the creases, and the limps, and the hard-earned joy as equals. For a simple moment, it will be thus. Then Pete will show me the way home, just as I have shown him whenever the privilege was given.

In Gratitude

IT TAKES A VILLAGE TO bring a book to life...and, as it turned out, a crazy little cattle dog from New Mexico. Thank you, Durango Pete.

My dad always said, "Your family is everything, son." He was right. Thank you to my children Gina, Krista, and Dallas. You are three blessings. Thank you to my partner and soulmate, Cynthia, who helped save Durango Pete, who certainly saved me, who gave me space and freedom to ramble and write. She is the nuts and bolts of this book.

Thank you Pauline Dube of Under My Wing in Moriarty, New Mexico. You saved Pete's life. You are an angel on earth.

A special thanks to Polly Letofsky whose expertise and encouragement got us from draft to delivery. Alexandra O'Connell was our editor extraordinaire. Victoria Wolf created our splendid cover design. Thank you Kristen Hellstrom, for loving Pete and for your help with the book photos.

Finally, thank you Joyce Leake and Tim 'The Trainer' Hartley. You helped unlock the mystery who is Durango Pete, a little cattle dog with a big attitude.

ABOUT THE AUTHOR

STEPHEN HINMAN CAME INTO THE world a hopeful wanderer, a ponderer of life, and a storyteller. After careers as an English teacher and coach, athletic club director, business owner, and physical therapist, Stephen made his way back to his early roots as a writer and poet.

Recently, he found a kindred spirit in his adopted cattle dog. Durango Pete, who has ancient wisdom, the gift of gab, and love of life, became Stephen's constant companion.

Stephen has 3 children and 5 grandchildren. He, Durango Pete, and his wife, Cynthia, split time between homes in Denver and Grand Lake, Colorado, where they frequent prairie and mountain trails and Stephen continues to write.

Let's Stay Connected

To STAY CONNECTED, PLEASE BE sure to find me online by visiting my web site at www.stephenhinman.com. Or connect with me on Facebook (Stephen Hinman) or Instagram (sshinman). You can also contact me via email at info@barkingcrowpublishing.com. I would love to hear from you.

To stay in touch with Durango Pete's continuing adventures, you can follow him on Facebook or Instagram.

And one last favor…

If you have enjoyed this book, please be sure to visit my Amazon book page and leave a review.

Thank you!

Made in the USA
Columbia, SC
21 October 2017